FIVE WORLDVIEWS
The Way We See the World

Dr. Denise R. Ames

Published in 2017 by Center for Global Awareness

ISBN: 978-1-943841-05-9

Book interior and cover design by Jeanine McGann
Background graphic image on front cover designed by Freepik.com
Photo collage on front cover designed by Jeanine McGann
Photo on back cover by Matthew Henry from unsplash.com under Creative Commons Zero license

The principal text of this book was composed in Gandhi Serif.

The Center for Global Awareness
Albuquerque, New Mexico, USA
www.global-awareness.org

Acknowledgments

I would like to thank several people in helping to bring this book project to fruition. First and foremost, as always, a special thanks to Nancy W. Harmon, my partner and board of directors member at the Center for Global Awareness. Her crisp editing, countless suggestions, and unfailing support have helped to make this book possible. Second, I would like to extend a special thanks to Jeanine McGann for her excellent work in formatting, editing, and getting the book ready for market. Her thorough work for the Center for Global Awareness is certainly appreciated and without her efforts, CGA would cease to operate efficiently.

Contents

Chapter 6. The Transformative Worldview

Preface

Worldviews have always fascinated me. Even though I hadn't yet conceptualized the idea of worldviews, instances in my life when there was a clear clash between worldviews alerted me to the different ways in which people react to different events. My father, a World War II veteran, and I, a rebellious college student, experienced heated clashes over opposing views of the Vietnam War in the 1960s. During my two-year residency in Mississippi in the 1970s, when a friendly neighbor first introduced herself, she asked me what Baptist Church I went to. She assumed I was a Baptist, since the church influenced her worldview. When I visited the Native American pueblo of Acoma in New Mexico in the 1980s, I was surprised to hear one of the visitor's criticize the pueblo's system of collective land-ownership. He grumbled that more money could be made dividing the land into individual plots and selling them off to the highest bidder. During the 1990s when globalization was heralded as the savior of the Western world, I found most people in the business community thought it was an inevitable process and could not be stopped, even though I and others had some misgivings about it. When I visited Iran in the 2000s, I was disturbed that the "culture police" could arrest me or any other woman for not dressing in the traditional way and looking too modern. All of these events and many others gave me glimpses into the different worldviews that people hold.

I first started to think about developing the concept of worldviews during my writing, teaching and research of my world history college course and the subsequent publication of my book, *Waves of Global Change: A Holistic World History*. In my teaching and book, I organized world history according to five waves of human development: communal, agricultural, urban, modern, and global. This was different from the traditional chronological format that organized world history according to the march of time rather than the less-sequential way of human development. But I also found that within each wave there was uneven development, and not everyone in each of the waves marched along to the same beat. I found this especially true with the Global Wave, which starts around the turn of the new millennium.

I found that during the Global Wave, there were many contentious and conflicting ways of seeing the world. Iranian fundamentalists established a theocracy in Iran after a revolution in 1979, while fundamentalists such as Pat Robertson were drawing many followers in the U.S. into the fold, mostly through television programming. The nationalistic fervor characteristic of the Modern Wave, which was supposed to decline with the upswing in globalization, was continuing and intensifying in the U.S. and other countries, even as the world was becoming more interconnected and global in scope. The traditions of the Communal and Agricultural Waves were being reasserted during this time, as many indigenous people resisted the pressure to modernize or let resources on their lands be exploited for extraction by multi-national corporations. The push for globalization, both economic and cultural, by the U.S. and other countries was a growing phenomenon that was supported politically, economically, and by the media. It appeared as an "inevitable" process, and we better jump on its bullet train of untold progress and riches or get left behind. Yet, there were those who resisted fundamentalism, modernism, and globalization and took action to create a different way of life. Although globalization supporters were garnering the most attention and putting forth an optimistic vision of the future, many other people were voicing different visions. But every individual has different ways of "seeing" events, facts, data, situations, people, movements, information, evidence, spectacles, and ways of living, which make the world appear as a very unpredictable and confusing place. Therefore, I decided that the Global Wave was not a homogenous view of the world, but that many differing views within it needed to be heard and recognized.

As a result of my research, observations, and experiences, I decided to organize the Global Wave into five worldviews—indigenous, modern, fundamentalist, globalized, and transformative. I thought it would be unwieldly to have more worldviews; I wanted my students and others to remember them, and the five worldviews coincided nicely with the five waves in my world history. I would use the term worldview since it most closely described the phenomena that I was identifying. I was attempting to show that each individual's reality is filtered through different lenses, and learning about these different lenses can help us improve communication and relations with people who are similar to and different from us.

Worldview is one of those terms that has multiple meanings and is often used inconsistently. I will be defining the term worldview as consisting of basic assumptions and images that provide a more or less coherent, though not necessarily accurate, way of thinking about the world. Worldviews are those systems or structures within which our values, beliefs, and assumptions lie. They influence how we see ourselves and others and how we make meaning of our lives and form relationships. Worldviews keep our lives coherent by giving us a sense of meaning, purpose, and connection.

When I started the Global Awareness Adult Conversation and Study Program, or Gather, I wanted to expand the typical way of studying global issues and cultural topics in which information is presented and acquired, to one in which participants would not only learn information but would develop an appreciation for the different ways in which individuals see the world. This approach would help participants evolve their own capacity for understanding others and encourage engagement in creating positive change. Thus, the four dimensions of SEEK emerged as see, evolve, engage, and know.

The 'see' dimension to me is a vital component in this program. Many of us live in a bubble, surrounded by people who have similar views on issues and comparable lifestyles, and who read the same books and listen to media that support our views. When we have a conversation about a controversial topic, we rarely hear conflicting views, which reinforces the notion that we are obviously right. Many of us rarely step outside our bubble to see other people's views. Even on some college campuses, the natural place for conflicting ideas, the speech of opposing voices is sometimes stifled because it is considered hostile, troublesome, or can "trigger" unpleasant emotions. This pattern of restricting behavior is detrimental to a democracy and hampers the interaction of different people in sustaining institutions that support a vibrant nation and economy.

The 2016 presidential election exemplified this "bubble phenomena." Many Hillary Clinton voters were stunned when there was a backlash among half of the voters against her liberal worldview in which minority rights were supported, preserving the environment was a priority, and a professional class of experts, not just billionaires, would help shape governmental policy. This dramatic and far-reaching electoral backlash exemplified the opposing ways in which half of the electorate saw issues through one lens while the other half saw issues very differently.

The See Dimension of the Gather program has been developed to try and make some sense of the multiple perspectives that are expressed by each person. Although the different "modes of seeing" that we explore in the See Dimension will not give a complete picture of reality, as this is impossible anyway, its purpose is to give an overview of several different lenses through which reality is perceived. From cross-cultural awareness, to systems thinking, cultural identity, individual personality traits, and worldviews, the many different lenses through which we see reality are explored.

This book will examine one of lenses through which we see reality: worldviews. The five worldviews—indigenous, modern, fundamentalist, globalized, and transformative—that I have developed and presented in this book are not the only way that we can see differences, but it is one of the lenses that help shape our perception of reality. Therefore, the worldviews book is just one mode of seeing that makes up the See Dimension. This book does not aim to neatly categorize all people into one of the categories, as you may find that you or others you know may identify with two or more worldviews. I know I do. But the book gives you a range of beliefs that are firmly held by a wide variety of people in the U.S. and the world.

The purpose of this book about worldviews is to help us become more aware of the diversity of thoughts and opinions that seem to be more prevalent today than in the past and to look into each other's worldviews without necessarily trying to change them. Since individuals may be very resistant to changing their worldview and resent those who try to do so, the point of learning about other worldviews is not to gain the tools to change another's worldview but to become aware of the existence of different worldviews and empathize with those holding differences. If we are aware of different worldviews, we may stop expecting "the other" to change his/her worldview and realize instead that "the other" makes sense of the world from his/her own worldview. In other words, we may find that the other side's outrageous or nonsensical ideas actually become reasonable and sensible when seen from their point of view.

Why do we need to be aware of others' worldviews? It is more comfortable to reside in our own bubble with people around us who have the same worldview, and our ideas and actions are unchallenged. But large, multi-ethnic, multi-cultural, and diverse countries like the United States, and increasingly many other countries around the world, are not homogenous entities, and this requires their citizens to engage with others to uphold democratic processes and peaceful co-existence. Citizens cannot remain in their own insulated bubble and still have a vibrant democracy. We all need to make an effort to gain the skills to navigate a more diverse world, which includes people from different lands as well as those who are our fellow citizens but live in a different state or zip code.

Becoming more aware of different worldviews and engaging with those who hold a different worldview is difficult and often descends into shouting matches, hateful language, vile stereotypes, bullying, and other forms of conflict. Conflict resolution processes need to help people look into each other's worldviews without trying to change them. It is possible to uncover shared values, or shared aspects of values, without fundamentally changing worldviews. Developing approaches to uncover shared values is an important area for development in conflict analysis and resolution. It is also one of the hoped-for end results of reading and discussing this book.

Understanding worldviews can be a resource for empathy and analyzing conflicts when fundamental differences divide groups of people. One of the ways to help express one's worldview is through the dialogic process of creating new or personal stories of how individuals came to their worldview and telling others about their heroes and heroines. In doing so, they reveal information about their identity, what they find meaningful, their ideas about the nature of life, relationships, and "right living." By listening deeply to other stories, we will find it harder to sustain negative images of the other, recognizing instead commonalities that had previously been unseen. From this base of empathy, individuals are able to explore shared values with more ease, while not losing sight of the aspects of values they do not share. Similarly, sharing stories of heroes helps participants glimpse into what is important to others and uncover values they share.

Awareness of worldviews with their embedded meanings can be the seedbed from which new, shared meanings emerge. These shared meanings may arise as people co-create new stories, as already mentioned, design new rituals, discover myths, find inclusive metaphors used by a group, and create new identities that lead participants to humanize each other even as they pursue their social and legal agendas about differing issues. As we positively engage with each other, we can learn efficiently and deeply about group members' identities (who they see themselves to be) and meanings (what matters to them and how they make meaning). When we do this with each party to a conflict, places of connection and divergence may become clearer, leading to a better understanding of the conflict in question.

When bridging the divide between two or more worldviews, a goal is to uncover universal, human commonalities that all people share despite differences. This may be easier said than done, but the process in the discovery is also a way to build bridges. A few of the universal commonalities that we all share include dignity and respect for all, the right to advocate for a point of view without fear of violence or reprisal, love and acceptance, security and safety, protection, incremental progress that improves lives, universal love and many more. The universal enjoyment of music, sports, entertainment, dance, and family is a shared interest that goes beyond differences and is a good subject for stories and conversations with those we perceive as different. We have more that binds us together than divides us.

When worldviews are not in our awareness or acknowledged, stronger parties in conflict may advertently or inadvertently try to impose their worldviews on us. Far more profound than trying to impose a particular solution to a conflict or a way of communicating, the imposition of a worldview can be destructive to a whole way of life. For example, judgments are one way in which one party tries to impose its worldview on another. Judgmental people who criticize and spread negative energy do this from the overflow of negativity that they have within them. When people label others as racist, bigoted, hateful, ignorant, homophobic, misogynists, baby-killers, murderers, white trash, or other hateful terms, the accuser is asserting that s/he has the moral high-ground and his/her values prevail. Those accused feel judged, demeaned, humiliated, and stripped of their dignity. When attacking those that seem to be in the wrong, the attackers must be aware that this assault is likely to make the situation even more extreme. If the purpose of attacking those we disagree with by using judgmental language is to change their behavior, the chances of doing so are significantly diminished by employing this tactic. Thus, the attacker's real purpose in using judgmental language is to shame the target population while thinking that s/he is morally superior.

When studying worldviews, it is helpful to realize that no one experiences reality directly. We all experience reality through our perceptual filters or our own lenses. We assign meaning to our experiences as they happen, and the meanings we give to our experiences are influenced by our attitudes and past experiences. It pays to remember that when we judge a situation—or when we assume something about someone else—we are doing this according to our perceptions of the event, not the actual event itself. Our worldviews may be hidden to us, but they are always active.

I hope you enjoy this book on worldviews as much as I have writing about, teaching, and researching the topic. If you are a member of the Global Awareness Adult Conversation and Study Program, Gather, please email us at info@global-awareness.org for the accompanying, free study guide. The purpose of our Gather program is to connect with others, to learn deeply, to unfold our hearts in empathy, to see with new eyes, and to activate our hands in engagement. Good luck to all of you!

Kind regards,
Denise R. Ames

CHAPTER ONE

Introduction to Five Worldviews:
The Way We See the World

"As the twig is bent, so grows the tree."

Why is it that one experience or situation can elicit so many different responses? Police often find that different eye witnesses can have wildly different interpretations of the same crime that their testimonies are virtually worthless in determining the outcome of a case. Proposals to demolish an old, decrepit building in the middle of a town can create a firestorm of reactions or the building of a Wal-Mart on the outskirts of town can raise the blood pressure of the entire community.

A contentious more global issue involves the rights of indigenous people to claim their artifacts. Natural history museums before 1990 often had exhibits depicting lands before European colonization. These exhibits often included artifacts and possibly skeletons of Native Americans; the tribes could claim no ownership rights to artifacts that were taken from their land. Their burial grounds were dug up by archaeologists, and the findings were dispersed to museums across the country and world. Many artifacts were either purchased, often below the value of the object, or stolen, with little legal recourse for the Native groups. Although these exhibits may be informative to the museum-goer, many Native Americans see them as a source of resentment. This changed in 1990 when the federal government passed the Native American Graves Protection and Repatriation Act, which gave them the legal authority to reclaim artifacts from feder-

Native headdress

ally funded museums. Museums are often asked to return objects that are sacred, meaning they are used in present-day ceremonies. Institutions also must give back artifacts that have "ongoing historical, traditional, or cultural importance central to the Native American group or culture itself." Tribes can claim ownership of the objects, and if a review determines their claim is justified, ownership of the artifact is given to the tribes. However, the question remains, "Who should own Native American artifacts?"[1] The essence of the question is also being asked globally. Should Egypt be able to request the return of their plundered antiquities from the British Museum in London or the Berlin Museum? It is not the purpose of this example to answer this question but to show that how one answers this question reflects, in part, one's particular worldview.

WORLDVIEWS: A DEFINITION

A **worldview** is a way of understanding or a lens through which one explains events, phenomena, and actions that happen in our everyday lives. It refers to the framework of ideas and beliefs through which an individual interprets the world and interacts with it. The term worldview comes from the German word *Weltanschauung*: *welt* means world and *anschauung* means outlook or view. A useful way to think of how a worldview shapes our reality is to think of a pair of glasses. We can see through the glasses without actually being aware of them, yet the prescription of the glasses is focusing the world for us. So too are worldviews. Every book read, policy statement enacted, vote cast, problem solved, class taught, Congressional bill passed, religious sermon preached, the way children are raised, and even the approach used to write this book are shaped as much, if not more, by our worldview as by any objective data or analysis.[2]

A worldview is an overall perspective from which one sees and interprets the world; a set of simplifying suppositions about how the world works and what is seen and not seen. It is an internal collection of assumptions, held by an individual or a group that are firmly believed to be self-evident truths. These assumptions shape an individual's beliefs, ideas, attitudes, and values, which, in turn, affect behaviors and actions. A worldview is a paradigm, a fundamental way of looking at reality which functions as a filter. When people look through a  filter, such as a pane of colored glass, they usually see through it, rather than seeing it—as so with worldviews. It admits information that is consistent with our deeply held expectations about the world while guiding us to disregard information that challenges or disproves these expectations.[3] A worldview acts as a built-in "operating system."

Each of us has a worldview. It develops in part because we seek some understanding of our own significance. People desire certitude by which to live their lives. There are universal queries for understanding important aspects of life. Through the lens of our worldview an individual is able to answer these universal queries, such as the notions of the existence or nonexistence of the supernatural and a deity or deities; the origins of the universe and of human life; the source of morality and values and identification of what is good or evil; how to live one's life; the meaning of life and of death; and so on. To a greater or lesser degree, people are able to obtain reassurances from worldview coherency.

Worldviews are rarely brought out into the light of day, so people are not usually aware of them. They are hidden deep in our human consciousness, all the while quietly shaping our reactions to new ideas and information, guiding our decisions, and ordering expectations for the future. For example, our worldview guides us in answering questions such as is free trade good for the economy, is universal health care a human right, is our clan always right, or does land always have a monetary value. A worldview consists of basic assumptions and images that provide a more or less coherent, though not necessarily accurate, way of thinking about the world.

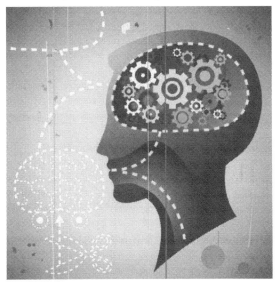

Subconscious mind

Worldviews deeply influence the kind of political, economic, cultural and social patterns we build, and those, in turn, reinforce the events that occur around the world. An iceberg serves as a good way to better understand worldviews. At the tip of the iceberg, the 10-20 percent seen above the surface represents events that occur around the world. These events are reported on the television news, headlined in the newspaper, or featured on the Internet. But looking beneath the surface level of the iceberg's events are the episodes.[4] For example, we see the event of Hurricane Katrina on the news, but the hurricane is not an isolated event; it is part of larger episodes of hurricanes that are wreaking havoc along coastlines. And if we look further below the surface of the iceberg's events and episodes, we see that a society's political, economic, technological, social, environmental, and cultural patterns have an impact on the events and episodes (I call these patterns "currents" in my holistic world history). Many scientists attribute such violent and extreme weather conditions as Hurricane Katrina to climate change, which is caused by our burning of fossil fuels. The modern economic system, the current or pattern, is based on the burning of fossil fuels for our energy consumption, which drives our modern way of life, while the environmental impact of burning fossil fuels is an unfortunate but necessary by-product.

Farther down towards the base of the iceberg are what I call worldviews, which, in turn, influence the events, episodes and patterns. Our worldview extols the idea that unlimited economic growth is the unquestioned path to prosperity and well-being. However, the environmental repercussions of this worldview are finally revealing the unintended consequences of this unquestioned belief in unlimited growth. Finally, at the very base of the iceberg we see the great mass of ice supporting the whole iceberg; these are our human behaviors, the universal human commonalities that shape who we are as a species. Therefore, if we want to change events, episodes and patterns we need to change our worldview that created them in the first place.

These worldviews are not merely the latest psychological profile fad but deeply entrenched mental constructs of how we see the world. They are the lens through which we make sense of reality, arrive at solutions to problems, create a way of living our lives, or structure our government and other institutions. In other words, we make both big decisions and little decisions through the lens of our worldview.

DEVELOPING AND PERPETUATING A WORLDVIEW

Much of any person's worldview is shaped by his or her culture and upbringing. But, a worldview is not merely a philosophical byproduct of a person's culture. Worldviews are constructed by society—that is, they are more collective than individual. I am also distinguishing worldviews from cultural views that I describe in another book. A worldview is a person's internal mental framework of cognitive understanding about reality and life meaning. No infant has a worldview. Each person's worldview takes shape over time as an individual grows and develops and as s/he engages in new events and experiences, interacts with others, and derives answers to inquiries about life and living from others.

Those involved in the early formation of a worldview for any child vary across cultural and other variables that influence a child's upbringing, such as living in a nuclear family or collective, extended family. In the United States, those who supply answers to questions and facilitate the formation of a youngster's worldview are usually parents and/or close family of the child. Their influence during formative years is powerful. Youngsters hold to their formulation of a worldview with varying degrees of firmness and cognitive maturity. Influences in modern society such as television, social media, and pop culture have an increasing bearing on worldview formulation and outcome.[5]

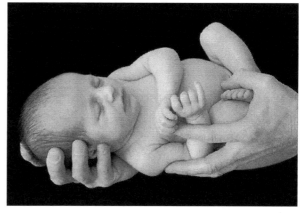

Those involved in shaping a youngster's worldview hope to produce a preferred outcome by exposing him/her to selected experiences and providing instruction by way of narratives, rituals and behaviors. This indoctrination process may involve screening out alternative worldview narratives and experiences, or at least careful managing of a youngster's acquaintance with them. Even a broad-minded approach, one which does not seek to restrict exposure to alternate worldviews, will involve instilling certain interpretations and offering guidelines that direct youngsters to accept a particular worldview. These guidelines may be regarded as helpful for understanding the universe, living life well, and gaining meaning, but the unconscious intention is to frame the youngster's worldview.

The process of education, by its very nature when conducted in public and private schools instills a particular worldview. Public education in the U.S. concentrates on interpreting the world in secular fashion according to authenticated, scientific standards of knowledge and molding conduct around common values of civilized society and a respect for individualism. The authentication process involves training experts in the peer-accepted standards of scientific knowledge and research. Religious schools may accept some of the scientific standards of knowledge found in the public schools, but also infuse religious ways of knowing that may conflict with scientific standards.

Chinese students, photo Denise Ames

For those instilling a worldview, the picture is more complicated than in the past. No longer can a family readily control major interactions of the child within a general locale and accepting local mores. The complexity and rapid changes within today's culture are bringing many more factors to bear. Technological developments and advertisers of a commercial marketplace may increasingly hold sway in shaping a youngster's worldview. The contemporary situation presents intense conflicts for those parents who seek a high degree of command over shaping their child's worldview. Even the most liberal of parents may be challenged by an inability to channel experiences for their progeny toward what they hold as a hoped-for outcome.

If worldviews are so important in influencing what we do, what are the prevailing worldviews that we all hold so dearly?

CONTEMPORARY WORLDVIEWS

A unique period of human history is occurring at this time, a fifth turning—what I have called the **Global Wave**—that is transforming our human story as this new millennium dawns. The Global Wave, as outlined in my book, *Waves of Global Change: A Holistic World History*, is characterized by rapid technological, intellectual, psychological, spiritual, economic, social, cultural, political, and ecological changes that are profoundly altering familiar patterns of the past. As is often the case when deep changes occur, there is today a great deal of anxiety, tension, conflict, and disruption as well. The deep changes occurring today are organized in this holistic world history into a fifth wave, the Global Wave. Deep transformations are not new in our human history, for punctuations of human rhythms have shifted the flow of history in the past as well. Periods of discontinuity alter the balance of continuity and create change. Now, once again, is a time of ground-breaking change.

Within the Global Wave there is not one all-pervasive, homogenous way of thinking and seeing reality. Instead I have identified five often contentious and conflicting worldviews with contradictory ways of knowing and understanding the world, each promoting dissimilar visions for the present and future. In the United States and throughout the world, most people identify with one or another of these worldviews or hold a combination of ideas from these five worldviews. The following is a brief summary of the five major worldviews: indigenous, modern, fundamentalist, globalized, and transformative. A more detailed description is found in the next five chapters.

1. An Indigenous Worldview

Very few people today hold an **indigenous worldview**. Indigenous peoples share a similar ethnic identity and usually inhabit a geographic region with which they have had an early historical connection. "Indigenous" means "from" or "of the original origin." Other terms used to describe indigenous peoples are aborigines, first people, native people, or aboriginal, but the United Nations prefers the term, "indigenous peoples." The world population of indigenous peoples is hard to estimate, but recent counts range from 300 million to 350 million. This would be just under 5 percent of the total world population. This number includes at least 5,000 distinct peoples in over 72 countries.[6]

Indigenous peoples today live in groups ranging from only a few dozen to hundreds of thousands or more. Many groups have declined in numbers and some no longer exist, while others are threatened. Modern populations have assimilated some indigenous groups, while in other cases they are recovering or expanding their numbers. Some indigenous societies no longer live

!Kung hunter

The Global Wave: Five Worldviews

Worldview	Indigenous	Modern	Fundamentalist	Globalized	Transformative
Views and Beliefs	connections, nature's ways, intangible, continuity, cyclical, very slow, live out, relationships, integration, holistic, collective, spiritual expression	individualism, competition, certainty, tangible, Newtonian machine, separation, categories, division, compartments, stages of development, predictable, orderly, chronological, linear	divine certainty, inspiration, moral certitude, unquestioning, dogma, creed, concrete representation, absolute, irreducible, literal, exact, devout, strident	individualism, scientific inquiry, Einstein relativity, uncertainty, irrational, competition, struggle, instantaneous, fragmented, opportunity, warp speed	interdependence, limits to science, organic, possibility, imagination, systems thinking, holistic, compassion, collective, deliberative, understanding, support, complementarity, synergy, process, integration, cyclical
Political Views	tribal wars, conflict scarce resources, tribal governing, councils, elders' wisdom, mediation	private ownership, nation-state, liberalism, socialism, communism, conquest, warfare, punishment, struggle	conservative, prescribed order, hierarchical, theocracy, deference to authority, battle unbelievers, punishment, discipline	corporate influence, warfare scarce resources, dollar democracy, intellectual property, punish "underachievers," short-term thinking	participatory democracy, community networks, self-organizing, defensive conflict, conflict scarce resources, dialogue, long term thinking
Economic Views	reciprocity, redistribution, local trade & distribution, domestic economy	capitalism (mercantilism, classical, regulated), socialism/communism, economic growth, mass production, individual ownership, labor unions	market fundamentalism, market is the "god," neoliberalism, economic growth, corporate capitalism	neoliberal capitalism, state capitalism, privatization, patents, commodification, hyper consumerism, economic growth	mixed economy, public ownership/commons, domestic economy, worker owned cooperatives, local agriculture & businesses, non-profit sector
Cultural Views	traditional wisdom, folk religions, animistic, ancestor worship	scientific method, reason, logic, reducible, faith in science, progress, secular, rational religion	faith in revealed truth, holy book authority, belief in science if not in conflict with divine truths, religious exclusivity	religion irrelevant, cutthroat competition, commodification of culture, social relations, individualism	spiritual, inclusive religious groups, multi-cultural, faith in people, collective, unity within diversity
Environmental Views	nature alive, natural rhythms, faith in nature, rooted in place	nature inanimate, exploit nature as commodity, nature limitless	nature is God's dominion, nature subdued for humans, nature is God's creation, humans preserve it	nature commodity, conflict scarce resources, environmental limits	sustainability, nature animate, earth-based connections, nature's limits
Social Views	customs, traditions, egalitarian, kinship bonds, community, elders' wisdom, exclusivity, local	intolerant "other," nuclear family, racism, social classes, hierarchy, patriarchy, mass education, national history, individualism	theocracy, patriarchy, hierarchy, own religious tribe, religious education, history based on religious beliefs, tenets	nuclear family, consumption family, privatized education, education for global competition	relationships, inclusive networks, reinvention of family, global community, holistic education, holistic world history

on their ancestral land because of migration, relocation, forced resettlement or having their land taken by others. In many cases, indigenous groups are losing or have lost their language and lands and have experienced intrusion and pollution of their lands and disruption of their traditional ways.

2. A Modern Worldview

A **modern worldview** traces its history back more than 500 years to the expansion of Western European power and influence around the world. The modern worldview has been especially powerful over the last two centuries and has today expanded to the farthest reaches of the world.

A modern worldview continues today as a way of understanding the world and solving problems. It has ushered in a host of astonishing achievements such as the equality of women, medical breakthroughs, technological

successes, educational progress, a high material standard of living

Modern Worldview

upholds scientific reasoning
praises individualism
treats nature as a commodity
promotes liberal political traditions
separates church and state
encourages industrial production
places faith in technological solutions

for some, and the advancement of human rights. But it has also promoted terrible failures, such as values of rampant consumerism, cut-throat competition, unlimited economic growth, the use of punishment as a way to correct behaviors, military force to resolve conflict, exploitation of the environment, and individualism over community.

3. A Fundamentalist Worldview

Fundamentalism is a strict belief in a set of principles that are often religious. Many who hold to these ideas wish to defend what they see as traditional religious beliefs of the past. Although fundamentalists believe they are following the exact traditions of the past, this would be impossible in

Industrial machine

a modern society. Instead their beliefs have grown out of a rejection of modern ideas along with a response to the unsettling effects of globalization. They see their religion as true and others as false. There are fundamentalist sects in almost all of the world's major religions, including Christianity, Islam, Hinduism and Judaism. Across cultures, fundamentalists share several common character-

istics, including a factual reading of scripture, a mistrust of outsiders, a sense of separation from modern culture, and a belief in the historical correctness of their religion. Some religious fundamentalists are politically active, trying to shape the political and social order in line with their beliefs. Many feel that the state should be run according to religious principles. Fundamentalists see the choices for organizing their nation as limited to a Western/modern society or a traditional society. Since they reject a modern society, the only other choice they see is the continuation of their traditional ways. Also many people in modern nations find that their traditional values give comfort and security in a rapidly changing and complex world.

Iranian women, photo Denise Ames

4. A Globalized Worldview

A fourth worldview, a **globalized worldview**, is sweeping the world today. It has grown out of the modern worldview and has many of its characteristics. But one of the differences is that in the globalized worldview "time has speeded up" and the pace of growth and development has spread to the farthest reaches of the earth. A globalized worldview affects all aspects of society and individuals' daily lives.

McDonald's Mega Mac in Malaysia

Globalized Worldview

interconnections
blurred boundaries, approximation
speed, networks, diversity
differentiation, specialization
productivity, consolidation
mergers, acquisitions
interdependence

In a globalized worldview, global capitalism is the dominant economic system. One global economic system governed by capitalist principles has enveloped national and local economies that governments have regulated and protected in the past. A global economic marketplace conducts business, currency exchanges, and trade policies that ignore national boundaries. Global multinational corporations make many of the economic rules and conduct the business of the world marketplace. They promote a consumer-focused economy and support a powerful financial sector. As we will find out, the globalization process, and in particular economic globalization has both negative and beneficial aspects.

5. A Transformative Worldview

At this point in time, diverse people are actively challenging the negative parts of the four other worldviews. These people say a different worldview or a different story is needed to make sure our human species and life as we know it on earth continue. Leaders from diverse fields – religious leaders, students, entrepreneurs, international political leaders, indigenous farmers, political activists, environmentalists, entertainers, scientists, working people, artists, writers, academics, educators, economists, concerned citizens, and others – are contributing to the creation of what I call a **transformative worldview**.

Critics say that none of the other worldviews are able to meet the challenges of the 21ˢᵗ century. For example, some think that fundamentalist beliefs will not help build a more culturally tolerant atmosphere in an increasingly interracial world. Yet, they admire the sense of community fundamentalists support. Some people advancing a transformative worldview admire the sense of local place and the importance of the environment that many

Organic farmers in Mexico, photo Denise Ames

indigenous people have connected with for millennia but don't want to lose a shared awareness as global citizens. Some people say that we need to move beyond the modern worldview without losing the value of scientific inquiry and rational, logical thought. Many people supporting a transformative worldview admire the advances in technology, transportation and communication, while rejecting the despoiling of our planet. They draw upon the globalized worldview idea that we are all global citizens yet want to limit the dominance of the world's economy by giant, multinational corporations.

Transformative Worldview

embraces cultural diversity
resists corporate dominance
questions consumerist values
supports collective efforts
advocates for more equal distribution
of wealth and power
encourages sustainability
emboldens progressive education
lobbies for worker-owned businesses

Indigenos Worldview	Modern Worldview	Fundamentalist Worldview	Globalized Worldview	Transformative Worldview
nature	scientific method	holy book authority	scientific inquiry	limits to science
faith in nature	faith in science	faith in revealed truth	faith in markets	faith in people
traditional wisdom	scientific certainty	divine inspiration	theory of relativity	systems thinking
tradition	progress	unquestioning	irrational	unity within diversity
stream of conscious	reason, logic	dogma	probability	consciousness
flux	autonomous, separate	consistent	instantaneous	simultaneity
the group	the individual	the fellowship	the consumer	global community
community	stages of development	hierarchical structure	fragmented	holistic
flows	compartmentalization	divisions	opportunity	networks
exclusivity of group	intolerant, "the other"	religious exclusivity	class exclusivity	inclusive
emotion	reason	passion	flashes of insight	compassion
ambiguous	reducible	irreducible	uncertain	relative
changelessness	objective thinking	absolutes	subjective thinking	understanding
intangible	tangible	literal	abstract	organic
nature alive	nature inanimate	nature subdued	nature as commodity	nature included
extended family	nuclear family	religious family	consumer family	community networks
egalitarian	order, hierarchy	unchanging order	arbitrary	complementarity
kinship bonds	racial discrimination	religious intolerance	class separation	multi-cultural
reciprocity	economic growth	modern economy	hyper growth	steady state
story	debate	sermon	discussion	conversation
harmony	conquest	conversion	market conversion	synergy
group democracy	liberalism	theocracy	elite democracy	participatory
tribal wars	war for conquest	holy war	terrorism	self-defense
conflict over scarcity	struggle, war	battle unbelievers	cutthroat competition	conflict over scarcity
cyclical	chronological, linear	teleological	virtual	spiral
hand-crafted	mass-production	household economy	efficiency, growth	community economy
ban from group	punish non-comformity	punish heretics	punish underachievers	support, nourish
learn from nature	mass education	religious education	privatized education	holistic education
folk religion	rational religion	universal religions	question religion	spiritual values

WORLDVIEWS: A TOOL FOR UNDERSTANDING OTHER PERSPECTIVES

When worldviews are not in our awareness nor acknowledged, stronger parties with more dominant worldviews may advertently or inadvertently try to impose their worldviews on others. Therefore, understanding worldviews can be a tool for recognizing and analyzing conflicts and tensions when fundamental differences divide groups of people. When each side of a conflict is understood according to their particular worldview, places of connection and divergence may become clearer, leading to a better understanding of the conflict or situation.

Worldviews, with their embedded meanings, can be the seedbed from which new shared meanings may emerge. By looking at the stories, rituals, myths, and metaphors used by a group of people holding a dissimilar worldview, we can learn efficiently and deeply about their worldview and what matters to them and how they make meaning. These shared meanings may arise as people co-create new stories, design new rituals, establish shared values, and find inclusive metaphors. In any given contentious debate or conflict, established societal values, such as security, family, and responsibility, will

Burning rituals

emerge. Because people relate to these values differently when they hold different worldviews, misunderstandings and negative judgments about "the other side" may follow. As people become aware of the existence of different worldviews, they may stop expecting "the other" to make sense of the way they perceive the world, and realize instead that "the other" makes sense of the problem from their own worldview. In other words the other side's perceived outrageous or nonsensical ideas may actually become reasonable and sensible when seen from their point of view.[7]

A Clash of Worldviews: the Abortion Debate

This section is an example of recognizing common values and shows the existence of divergent worldviews in conversations between advocates on both sides of the abortion conflict in Canada and the United States.

Both pro-life and pro-choice advocates value benevolence, universalism, and security, but their worldviews lead them to see these values differently. Pro-life advocates, for example, may see all life as sacred from the moment of conception and suggest that no human being should second-guess God or the Universe in its life-creating and life-ending capacity. Their idea of benevolence thus extends

Pro-life demonstrators

to the unborn fetus as well as to the other people involved in an unwanted or unplanned pregnancy. Pro-choice advocates are no less benevolent, but are apt to focus their efforts to improve and enhance welfare for those already born. Their worldview may place more credence in science or involve a different notion of when human life begins, such as at the point the fetus is viable outside the womb or when a woman first discerns life within.

Part of the reason that the abortion debate has become so heated and volatile is that it is bound up with social and legal rules. Both sides would like their views to be universal, at least within the countries of Canada or the United States. Many pro-life advocates argue against public funding for, or provision of, abortion services. Many pro-choice advocates argue for public funding and universal availability of these services. As these two directions for universal application of norms, standards, and public services have clashed, the intractable conflict between the two sides has escalated. The value of security also plays out in the pro-life/pro-choice conflict. Pro-life advocates are concerned about the security of unborn children and the families into which they are born. Pro-choice advocates focus on the security of those involved with unwanted and unplanned pregnancies. While both are concerned with security, they differ in some important ways on what security means.

How did pro-choice and pro-life advocates come to see each other's worldviews, thus building a base of respect for each other that was broad enough to support dialogue and discover shared values? Dialogues convened by the Network for Life and Choice in Buffalo, New York helped pro-life and pro-choice advocates become aware

Pro-choice demonstrators

of their differing worldviews, and made the process of uncovering shared aspects of values possible. The facilitators asked participants to do two things that helped reveal their worldviews. They were asked to share personal stories of how they came to their views and to tell each other about their heroes and heroines. In doing so, they revealed things about their identity, what they found meaningful, their ideas about the nature of life, relationships, and "right living." Listening to these stories, the dialogue participants found it harder to sustain negative images of the other, recognizing instead commonalities that had previously been closed to them. From this base of empathy, they were able to explore shared values with more ease, while not losing sight of the aspects of values they did not share. Similarly, sharing heroes helped participants see what was precious to others and find values they shared.

Through dialogue, advocates from pro-life and pro-choice perspectives came to see that they shared some values. Both sides agreed about some aspects of security—for example that action to alleviate female and child poverty is desirable and necessary. Similarly, both pro-life and pro-choice advocates agreed on benevolence in the form of adoption services and on ways to limit behavior outside clinics that might hurt or intimidate. They also agreed that some values should be universal: dignity and respect for all, including the right to advocate for a point of view without fear of violence or reprisal.

As mentioned above, those with different worldviews may find shared meanings as they co-create new stories, design new rituals, and find inclusive metaphors. One of the ways that the pro-choice and pro-life advocates came to see these shared values was through the dialogic process of creating new stories and new identities. Participants in ongoing pro-choice/pro-life dialogue groups reported no diminishment of their ardor as advocates, but they did report that they assumed additional identities as participants in the dialogue. These new identities led them to humanize each other even as they pursued their social and legal agendas about the issue of abortion and ways of dealing with unwanted, unplanned pregnancies.[8]

ALTERING A WORLDVIEW

Worldviews influence how we see ourselves and others and how we make meaning of our lives and relationships. Since resolving conflict and negotiating through a multi-cultural, complex world necessarily involves some kind of change or accommodation, it is essential to understand the operation of worldviews. When people are asked to change their worldview, identity or what they find meaningful, they will often resist. Worldviews keep our lives coherent, giving us a sense of meaning, purpose, and connection. Conflict resolution processes need to help people look into each other's worldviews without trying to change them. As illustrated by the abortion dialogue example, it is possible to uncover shared values without fundamentally changing worldviews. Developing approaches to uncover shared values is an important area for future development in conflict analysis and resolution.

As long as life continues to be lived, a worldview is susceptible to alteration. An adult's worldview may, but need not, remain consistent. As a person precedes through his/her life there may

be events that compel a radical reformation of outlook. For example, exposure to new ways of thinking through education may induce varying degrees of a changed perspective. Vivid experiences or persuasive encounters may engender dramatic alteration of outlook. Exposure to different cultural practices or mores, or changes in geography or living circumstance, or significant tragedy or success—such experiences may revamp one's way of thinking about life and meaning.[9]

Purposeful attempts to modify another person's worldview may not be successful. Stress and internal conflict (for the one who is the target) may show up in such an endeavor. For example, when an educator teaching evolution challenges a student who believes in creationism the result may be that the student resists or opposes the intrusion. Even a person intimidated or persecuted to change his/her worldview may privately hold fast to his/her outlook. Presenting facts that reinforce a particular worldview does little to persuade others to change their worldview to the one that is perhaps more factually accurate.[10]

COMPONENTS FOUND IN ALL WORLDVIEWS

Worldviews have common components. It is important to keep these in mind as you establish your own worldview and as you share with others:

1. Absolutes. This is a value or principle that is regarded as universally valid or that may be viewed without relation to other things; good and evil are presented as absolutes. Examples of this concept include democracy is the best government, individualism is better than collectivism, power always corrupts, competition leads to best outcomes, and economic growth is essential.

2. Infinite Reference Point. Although many will try to deny this fact, all of us seek an infinite reference point. Whether it is God, science, power of the Universe, Man, the nation/state, agnosticism, love, mother Earth, the United States is an evil empire, government is always bad, the police are racist, blacks are lazy, or other types of reference points, arguments fall back on this point.

3. Faith. All of us presuppose certain things to be true without absolute proof. There are many inferences or assumptions upon which a worldview is based. This becomes important, for example, when we interact with those who claim that only science is completely neutral or objective. Some

Mother Earth

common assumptions underlying worldviews are: a personal God exists, man evolved from inorganic material, man is essentially good, reality is material, beliefs form our behaviors, and science is unalterable.

4. Provides Meaning. All worldviews provide meaning to those who hold fast to their principles. A New Age adherent firmly believes that science does not hold all the answers, but quantum waves of energy shape our destiny. Those protesting social injustice believe they have the moral high ground in supporting the downtrodden. Donald Trump supporters believe that a "strong man" can most effectively help their lives. Many righteously hold onto their "true" meanings.

Even though the globalized worldview seems to have emerged as the most dominant at this time, I have come to the conclusion that none of the worldviews will disappear. If this is so, it means that it will behoove all of us to understand and learn to negotiate with people holding different worldviews in order to have a more peaceful, tolerant and viable future. We all have a voice and a critical stake in the future outcome.

CHAPTER TWO

The Indigenous Worldview

Treat the earth well: it was not given to you by your parents,

it was loaned to you by your children.

We do not inherit the Earth from our Ancestors,

we borrow it from our Children.

— Ancient Proverb

THE INDIGENOUS WORLDVIEW: AN INTRODUCTION

The indigenous worldview is held by very few people today. **Indigenous peoples** are any ethnic group who share a similar ethnic identity and inhabit a geographic region with which they have the earliest known historical connection.[1] The adjective "indigenous" has the common meaning of "from" or of the "original origin." Therefore, in a sense any given people, ethnic group or community may be described as being indigenous in reference to some particular region or location. Indigenous peoples are usually a politically underprivileged group, whose ethnic identity is different from the nation in power and who have been an ethnic entity in the locality before the present ruling nation took over power.[2] Other terms used to describe indigenous peoples are aborigines, first people, native people, aboriginal, or Native Americans or Indians in the U.S. However, the preferred term, indigenous peoples, appears to be used by different international agencies such as the United Nations and will be used here.

Aboriginal people, Australia

Indigenous societies are found in every inhabited climate zone and continent of the world from small farming villages in India and Africa, to Native American pueblos in the Southwestern United States, to farming and herding communities high in the Himalayas, to nomadic groups in the African savannah, and to remote groups in the far Arctic reaches of Canada and Alaska. Indigenous societies range from those who have been significantly exposed to modern influences such as the Maya peoples of Mexico and Central America to those who as yet remain in comparative isolation from any external influence such as the Sentinelese and Jarawa of the Andaman Islands in the Bay of Bengal to the east of India.

The total world population of indigenous peoples is hard to estimate given the difficulties of identification and inadequate census data, but recent estimates range from 300 million to 350 million as of the start of the 21st century. This would be just under 6 percent of the total world population. This total number includes at least 5,000 distinct peoples in over 72 countries.[3]

Indigenous peoples today survive in populations ranging from only a few dozen to hundreds of thousands or more. Many groups have undergone a dramatic decline and some have even gone extinct, while others remain threatened. Some groups have also been assimilated by other modern populations, while in other cases indigenous populations are undergoing a recovery or expansion in numbers. Some indigenous societies no longer live on the land of their ancestors because of migration, relocation, forced resettlement or having their land taken by others. In many cases, the changes for indigenous groups are ongoing and include permanent loss of language, loss of lands, intrusion onto traditional territories, pollution of traditional lands, and disruption in traditional ways of life.

In the past and even today, many indigenous peoples have been subject to intense discrimination by Europeans or other people holding a modern worldview. The modern societies, who held superior warfare technology and immunity to deadly diseases, derisively labeled indigenous people as primitive, inferior, savage, uncivilized, backward, undeveloped, ignorant, and other derogatory terms. Through education and greater awareness, these labels have been largely jettisoned and replaced with terms such as indigenous peoples, which do not hold an evaluative judgment of superior or inferior.

Even though their number is small and the modern perception of inferiority still continues among some, inclusion of their worldview is important in the Global Wave. Since they have successfully survived for thousands of years compared to modern society that has continued for a mere 500 years, they have much wisdom to share with all of us.

Because of the systematic destruction of indigenous cultures by Western nations during the Modern Wave

Inuit family, Alaska, USA

(1500 onward), the United Nations (UN) has taken up their cause with the UN General Assembly adoption of the **Declaration on the Rights of Indigenous Peoples** in September 2007, a process stretching back to 1982. The non-binding declaration outlines the individual and collective rights of indigenous peoples, as well as their rights to identity, culture, language, employment, health, education and other issues. Four nations with significant indigenous populations voted against the declaration: the United States, Canada, New Zealand and Australia. In 2004, the United Nations General Assembly declared 2005-2014 to be the Second International Decade of the World's Indigenous People. The main goal during this decade will be to improve international cooperation around resolving the problems faced by indigenous peoples in areas such as culture, education, health, human rights, the environment, and social and economic development.[4]

The United Nations has not adopted any official definition of "indigenous" considering the diversity of indigenous peoples. Instead the UN has developed an understanding of indigenous based on the characteristics in the box to the right:[5]

One characteristic of indigenous people is that they reached a social and technological plateau hundreds to thousands of years ago, although many have recently adopted modern technology so this characteristic may no longer apply. Many indigenous

Indigenous People

1. Self-identification as indigenous peoples at the individual level and accepted by the community as their member
2. Historical continuity with pre-colonial and/or pre-settler societies
3. Strong link to territories and surrounding natural resources
4. Distinct social, economic or political systems
5. Distinct language, culture and beliefs
6. Form non-dominant groups of society
7. Resolve to maintain and reproduce their ancestral environments and systems as distinctive peoples and communities.

17

groups rely upon subsistence production based on pastoral (herding), horticultural (simple agriculture) and/or hunting and gathering techniques. Many live in non-urbanized societies, although this is changing as well. Indigenous societies may be either settled in a given locale or region or follow a nomadic lifestyle.

A few indigenous people continue to observe an ancient hunting and gathering or foraging way of life in which their material possessions are few. Following a nomadic way of life, they must rely on nature for all of their material wants and needs. Their social structure is usually egalitarian with women having equal status, their kinship bonds are strong, and elders are respected as wise leaders. This all but disappearing way of life is practiced by people such as the !Kung in southwest Africa and Mbuti in the forest regions of the Congo who have continued their traditional ways for thousands of years. Herders who move their camps in order for their animals to feed on fresh pastures are also

!Kung village, Africa

indigenous peoples. Some still survive on the Mongolian steppes, but their way of life is also rapidly changing.

Indigenous people who follow simple agricultural techniques and live in small village settings and herders who move their camps in order for their animals to feed on fresh pastures are included in the indigenous worldview. Although many traditional agricultural people have historically been self-sufficient in supplying their own food and other needs, this way of life is being eroded by the increasing commercialization and globalization of agriculture and animal husbandry with

the resulting migration of traditional people to cities in "underdeveloped" areas of the world. Some people in villages and herding camps have been able to survive by supplying the food needs of their village and group, but also working at jobs that pay a wage in order to purchase basic needs in the cash economy. Even though this "hybrid" approach does not replicate agriculture or herding people of the last several thousand years, many do struggle to preserve their cultural traditions, close family networks, and indigenous religious traditions as much as possible in face of mounting pressures from the "outside," globalized world.

Questions to Consider

1. Why do you think that indigenous peoples have been maligned and slaughtered by modernizers?

CLASHING WORLDVIEWS: MODERN AND INDIGENOUS

"...it seemed a part of her life, to step from the ancient to the modern, back and forth. She felt rather sorry for those who knew only one and not the other. It was better, she thought, to be able to select from the whole menu of human achievements than to be bound within one narrow range."

— Orson Scott Card, *Children of the Mind*

Indigenous people have been under pressure over the last hundred years, and especially since the end of World War II, to change their way of life to conform to modern ways of living, a process often called modernization. Although on the surface this seems like a simple switch, with traditional people acquiring a few additional material possessions that would presumably make their life more comfortable. However, modernization efforts profoundly change the indigenous deep-seated way of life. The following is an examination of the economic, social, religious, political, psychological, and environmental changes that traditional people undergo when adapting a modern way of life. Even though a full description of the modern worldview follows in the next chapter, a comparison of the modern and indigenous worldview highlights the stark differences between the two worldviews. With this comparison, we can better understand both the indigenous and modern ways of living and why many indigenous people have resisted modernization, and for those who have accepted modernization, the difficulties they face in making the transition to a different way of life.

Modern and Indigenous Economic Differences

Indigenous people are pressured by modernizers to change economically in several ways. The use of machine power instead of animal or human power shows moving from the simple use of technology to the complex use of technology. Since many indigenous people are farmers, there is

The Story of the Mexican Fisherman

An American banker was at the pier of a small coastal Mexican village when a small boat with just one fisherman docked. Inside the small boat were several large yellowfin tuna. The American complimented the Mexican on the quality of his fish and asked how long it took to catch them.

The Mexican replied, "Only a little while." The American then asked why he didn't stay out longer and catch more fish. The Mexican said he had enough to support his family's immediate needs. The American then asked, "But what do you do with the rest of your time?"

The Mexican fisherman said, "I sleep late, fish a little, play with my children, take siestas with my wife, Maria, stroll into the village each evening where I sip wine and play guitar with my amigos. I have a full and busy life." The American scoffed, "I am a Harvard MBA and could help you. You should spend more time fishing and with the proceeds, buy a bigger boat. With the proceeds from the bigger boat, you could buy several boats, eventually you would have a fleet of fishing boats. Instead of selling your catch to a middleman you would sell directly to the processor, eventually opening your own cannery. You would control the product, processing, and distribution. You would need to leave this small coastal fishing village and move to Mexico City, then LA and eventually New York City, where you will run your expanding enterprise."

The Mexican fisherman asked, "But, how long will this all take?"

To which the American replied, "15 – 20 years."

"But what then?" asked the Mexican.

The American laughed and said, "That's the best part. When the time is right you would announce an IPO and sell your company stock to the public and become very rich. You would make millions!"

"Millions – then what?"

The American said, "Then you would retire. Move to a small coastal fishing village where you would sleep late, fish a little, play with your kids, take siestas with your wife, stroll to the village in the evenings where you could sip wine and play your guitar with your amigos."[6]

a push for them to substitute tractors and gas-powered machines to do the work they traditionally did through their own human labor and harnessed animal power. Modernizers want farmers to become more productive and efficient in their farming methods and produce a more abundant crop, usually a commercial crop for the world market. But for small farmers to be more productive, one of the changes they must undertake is to use modern, labor-saving machinery. However, tractors and other farm machinery need technical expertise to maintain operations; therefore, farmers must be trained as mechanics or rely on outside mechanics to maintain the machinery for them. Also, fuel for the machines and the machines themselves must be purchased at world market prices; hence, farmers must in some way obtain cash by participating in the market place to purchase these necessary items for the market economy. Cash is usually earned by converting subsistence crop produc-

Sustainable, organic farming, Mexico, photo Denise Ames

tion to growing cash crops. The cash crops are in turn sold on the world market for world market prices that can fluctuate dramatically from year to year and even month to month.

The self-sufficient farmer does not need cash for farming and, therefore, does not borrow money from banks or other money lenders. But if the farmer participates in the global economy, cash is needed for machinery, seed, pesticides, fertilizers and more land to expand his farming operations. To borrow money the farmer needs some type of collateral for the bank loan. The only collateral available is usually his/her land that perhaps is part of collective land communally held by the group. Modernizers push traditional farmers to privatize their communal land into individual plots that now have a monetary value and can be bought and sold. If the farmer uses his privately held land for collateral for a loan, he faces the risk of losing it if his crops fail to bring in the needed revenue for repayment of the loan's principal and interest. Now, the formerly self-sufficient farmer is transformed into a farmer dependent on the world market forces and credit system for his livelihood.

Since market farming favors economies of scale, many small farmers are not able to make a living as market farmers and end up losing their land. Without a way to make a living, many reluctantly move from their traditional rural villages to large urban centers for jobs, and, most likely, from self-sufficiency to poverty status. Other unemployed small farmers seek work on large agricultural plantations that grow cash crops on a vast scale. They earn a low wage for their labor and live in housing, often squalid, provided by their absentee landowning employer.

Modern and Indigenous Social Differences

Indigenous people also experience profound change in their social relations. For example, in traditional societies social relationships tend to be personal and emotional, and interaction is face-to-face. Economic negotiations are conducted with the implicit purpose of maintaining a good social association and a person's word or handshake is a ritual for an agreed-upon transaction or agreement. In modern societies social relationships are neutral, impersonal, detached, and indirect. These social relations make it possible for efficient market associations to take place, while legal, written contracts replace the handshake or a verbal agreement as a way to seal a transaction.

The family has many responsibilities and serves as the multifunctional core for indigenous people. The family provides emotional support for all members, oversees marriage and reproduction, performs informal socialization and education, cares for the welfare of the elderly and young, conducts economic production, and performs religious functions. The modern family is small and nuclear and has very different and reduced functions and responsibilities compared to indigenous families. Education, religion, care of the elderly, and medicine are worth noting as four areas in which traditional and modern people differ.

Care for the young is outside the family, with specific institutions taking over the responsibility of formal education for children in order to prepare them for work in a market place economy on which they are dependent for their livelihood. Schools, either private or state-sponsored, provide care and education for children who are sometimes as young as a few weeks

Indigenous family, Brazil

old to young adults in graduate schools who are well into their 20s and beyond. Modern, formal educational practices, such as the push to eradicate illiteracy and introduce the young to scientific principles and Western values, are an effort to inculcate modernization ideals among indigenous people.

A !Kung woman, Africa, photo Izla K. Bardavid

Indigenous education that emphasizes self-sufficiency methods and traditional crafts and how to function in a traditional society has been devalued.

Indigenous families care for the elderly. The elderly are highly regarded for their wisdom and experiences and have a leadership role in the community. In contrast, modern societies have created the concept of retirement for the elderly. Around the age of 65, the elderly retire from their work and pursue a life of leisure and hobbies if financially able. Some head off to "retirement communities," where they live with other retirees, not their children, in a separated cocoon from the outside world. For some the retirement years are banal and unfulfilling and many yearn to be more productive members of their communities. The modern society emphasizes youth and youthful beauty, and often seniors are publicly ridiculed as senile or "out of touch." Older seniors are often separated into state or private corporate facilities designated especially for their care, often called nursing homes, where they are largely forgotten. The years of experience, leadership and wisdom of the elderly go largely untapped by younger modern generations of youth.

Modern and Indigenous Religious Differences

Religious functions in indigenous societies are closely tied to the village and families of the people they serve. Religious specialists such as shaman or healers traditionally performed religious rituals, healing ceremonies, and ancestor worship. Modernizers have often dismissed and ridiculed indigenous medicines and healing practices performed by shamans and healers, while modern medicines and practices are promoted. In modern societies, religious functions are the responsibility of institutions outside the family that are headed by individuals who are trained in educational institutions specifically for educating religious leaders. Modern nations vary in their support of religious institutions. For example, in the U.S. religious institutions do not pay taxes on their establishments.

Hamatsa shaman, Canada

Religious functions in indigenous societies are integrated into all aspects of community life. Religious specialists such as **shaman** or healers traditionally perform religious rituals, healing ceremonies, and guide the practice of ancestor worship. Religious modernizers have sought for hundreds of years to rid indigenous peoples of their traditional religions and impose one of the universal religions, such as one of the forms of Christianity, Islam, Judaism, or Buddhism. In order to appease their conquerors, many indigenous peoples have blended their traditional beliefs with one of the universal religions, a process called **syncretism**.

Altay shaman, Siberia

Modernizers have often dismissed and ridiculed indigenous medicines and healing practices performed by shamans and healers as superstitious and unscientific, while modern medicines and practices are promoted. This practice has been changing in recent decades, as practices such as Chinese medicine, acupuncture, massage, and shamanic healing have been shown to be beneficial to patients.

Modern and Indigenous Political Differences

The political changes from indigenous to modern societies are also quite disruptive. These changes involve replacing the traditional religious, family, and ethnic political authorities with a single, secular, national political leader. In other words, there has been a move to replace a decentralized, local political system with a modern, highly centralized government, complete with a large bureaucracy and written laws. Therefore, loyalty to the extended family and tribe has shifted to an allegiance to the state and political parties. A modern political system requires that diverse social groups come together to form working coalitions of different political parties. These parties then compete in a voting procedure for political rule with the winner selected as the elected leader. A large centralized government requires a large bureaucracy in order to function smoothly. Workers in the bureaucracy need to be formally educated in the functions of a modern state system. Often this education is obtained overseas in Western educational institutions, such as the United States or Europe. The educated elite return to their country of origin intent on changing the indigenous political system to what they consider a superior, modern system.

Bedouin warrior, Arabian peninsula

An impersonal, legal atmosphere is typical of modern political exchanges, which is usually alien to indigenous peoples.

Original Painting by David Williams, Tahlequah, Okla.

Native American tribes, USA

Untold numbers of indigenous people have been swindled of their land by intricate legal technicalities that they are unfamiliar with or that are not compatible with their worldview as to how agreements are conducted. In the United States in the 1890s, for example, native people, known as the Five Civilized Tribes, were displaced onto reservations in Oklahoma, according to the provisions of the Dawes Act of 1887. Eager white settlers rushed onto the tribes' territory to stake a proprietary claim on what they stated was "unsettled" land. Native people faced additional pressure to "give up" their land when oil was discovered on the Oklahoma parcels that were previously thought to be "worthless." Lawyers descended like locusts into Tulsa, Oklahoma, to defraud tribal people of their claim to land according to a corrupt legal system. Of course, the lawyers made a great deal of money in their deceitful endeavors.

Modern and Indigenous Psychological Differences

The psychological changes that accompany modernization are perhaps the most unsettling for indigenous individuals. Values that support modernization need to be inculcated by individuals and families instead of the traditional values that have served the community for generations. Probably the most significant change in values is the increased focus on self-orientation and **individualism**—the modern individual—rather than a focus on the collective or group orientation of indigenous peoples. The modern individual is socialized to be independent, active, and open to new experiences, interested in public policies and cultural matters, and to think about long-term plans for the future. The traditional individual is socialized to be more passive and accepts

Maasai warriors, Africa

23

the traditions of the group, thinks in the present and short-term, defers to the group's leaders, and is rooted to his/her local place. The modern individual has a mobile personality and readily changes and adapts to a rapidly changing world, even if it means relocating to a different place apart from his/her family. Modern individuals are socialized to strive for an achieved status—through educa-

Ainu people, Japan

tion and hard work—and understand that there is the potential to become something different in the future. Indigenous individuals willingly follow their ascribed status, which is the status they are born into.

An indigenous person often experiences the disruptive forces of modernization which tend to produce alienation, anomie, and psychological disintegration. **Alienation** is the state in which people feel separated or detached from their past experiences or their family or group. They are forced or pressured to create a new modern identity which can lead to physiological stress, often resulting in an increase in violence and conflict. For example, the increased incidences, especially among indigenous men, of alcoholism, drug addiction, and abuse of family members repeatedly accompany the transition from traditional to modern societies. One source of violence in the societies that are making the transition from traditional to modern is the significant gap between new aspirations that individuals strive for and their ability to satisfy these aspirations because they remain marginalized from mainstream society."

Modern and Indigenous Environmental Differences

A fundamental difference between modern and indigenous worldviews is their concept of land, subsistence, sustainability and land ownership. Those holding a modern worldview see land as a commodity that can be bought and sold, owned individually by private owners, and assigned a monetary value based on the laws of supply and demand. This commodification of land is in keeping with the modern economic views that have applied capitalist principles to every aspect of life. On the other hand, indigenous views of land are quite different. Land is collectively "owned" by the group with no individual private ownership, although families may farm the same plot of land over the years there is no concept that the land belongs to them. In countries with large indigenous populations, laws protect col-

Hunting expedition, !Kung, Africa

lective ownership. For example, in 9 of the 12 countries of South America at least 20 percent of the land is legally in indigenous and peasant hands under collective legal systems.[7]

Sustainability is a concept of resource preservation that is more compatible with the indigenous worldview than with the modern. Continuity is a practice guiding many indigenous beliefs (at least in the past) which means that there is not the impulse to exploit resources for growth and instant consumption, rather to preserve resources for future generations. A motto among many indigenous peoples is that all actions be guided by the well-being of future generations.

Questions to Consider

1. What lessons can we learn from the way that those promoting a modern worldview treated those who hold an indigenous worldview?

GROWING UP IN AN INDIGENOUS SOCIETY: THE STORY OF RIGOBERTA MENCHU

"We Indians never do anything which goes against the laws of our ancestors." — *Rigoberta Menchu*

This section tells the childhood story of **Rigoberta Menchu** growing up poor in the poor country of Guatemala. As an indigenous person with a culture different from modern culture, in a sense, she speaks for all indigenous peoples of the American continent. The cultural discrimination she has suffered is something that all the continent's indigenous peoples have been experiencing since the Spanish conquest. Her voice allows indigenous peoples to speak. She is a witness to discrimination who has survived the violence aimed at destroying her family, community and culture, and she is stubbornly determined to break the silence and to confront the systematic extermination of her people.

Rigoberta Menchu, 2009

Menchu belongs to the Quiche people (a branch of the Mayans), one of the largest of the 23 ethnic groups in Guatemala, each having its own language. She was born on January 9, 1959 in the hamlet of Chimel on the Altiplano (highlands) to a poor peasant family who lived in a village in the northwestern Guatemalan province of El Quiche. She was immersed in the Mayan culture. In her autobiography, *I, Rigoberta Menchu*, she tells the story of the Guatemalan people and her personal experiences, which are, in essence, the reality of a whole people. Colonial powers have historically oppressed her people, and she is determined to make sure that the sacrifices her family and community have made to fight this oppression will not have been in vain. She makes it clear that "Latin Americans are only too ready to denounce the unequal relations that exist between ourselves and North America, but we tend to forget that we too are oppressors and that we too are involved in relations that can only be described as colonial. In countries with a large Indian population, there is an internal colonialism which works to the detriment of the indigenous population."[8]

Indigenous people in a village

To Rigoberta Menchu living in the village of Chimel as a child was paradise. It had no big roads and no cars. People could only reach it by foot or horseback. Her parents moved to Chimel in 1960 and began cultivating the land. No one had lived there before because it was very mountainous, but they were determined to stay no matter how hard the life. They had been forced to leave their previous hometown because *ladinos* (Guatemalans of mixed Spanish and Indian ancestry) settled there and gradually took control. Her parents spent all they earned and accumulated so much debt that finally they had to leave their house to pay the *ladinos*.

Rigoberta's father had a very hard life as a child. His father died when he was a child, leaving his wife with three small boys to raise. Her grandmother went to work as a servant for the

town's only wealthy family. The boys did small jobs around the house, such as carrying wood and water and tending animals. As they grew into young men, her employer didn't want to keep feeding them, so her grandmother had to give away her eldest son, Rigoberta's father, to a man who fed and worked him. Her father soon left that situation and found a job on a plantation growing coffee, cotton, and sugar cane. He sent for his mother and brothers to live with him. They earned very little money but were able to finally save enough

Guatemalan coffee plantation

to move to the high country. Shortly after the move, her grandmother became ill and died. The brothers decided to split up and the army forcibly recruited her father.

After her father's discharge from the army, her parents met and soon after married. Her mother also came from a very poor family who lived in the Altiplano. They moved about looking for work in the area and were hardly ever at home. Her parents got permission from the government and scraped together enough money to pay a fee to cultivate land in the Altiplano. Since it took many long, hard years for the land to finally produce crops, her parents had to travel down to the coastal region to work on the plantations.

The family grew rapidly; Rigoberta was the sixth of nine children. Like other indigenous families, the children suffered from malnutrition. Most children didn't reach the age of 15 years old. When she was a little girl she remembered spending only 4 months in the family's house in the Altiplano and the rest of the year working on the coastal plantations. Only a few families owned the vast plantations producing cash crops that were sold abroad. Poor families like the Menchu's tended the crops, a harsh life that her parents and others endured for many years.

In Menchu's community there was a highly respected elected representative who acted as a father to the whole village. Her mother and father were the village's representatives and the mother and father for all the children of the village. The birth of a baby is very significant for the community, as it belongs to all, not just the parents. Her mother, a midwife, helped women give birth at home; villagers considered it a scandal to have a child in the hospital. The community baptized a newborn before the parents took the infant to church. The newborn's hands were tied for eight days, which symbolized that one should not accumulate things the rest of the community does not have. On the eighth day the child's hands were untied; the open hands meant s/he knew how to share and be generous. The family teaches each child to live like fellow members of his/her community; no one had more than others.

Rigoberta's fellow villagers were Catholic, but they saw the religion as just another channel of spiritual expression. They didn't totally trust all the priests, monks, and nuns of the church. They believed that the sun was the father, and mother was the moon. Rigoberta felt that the Catholic Church has tried to "keep her people in their place," but as Christians they gradually acquired an understanding of their rights and dignity. She thinks "that unless a religion springs from within the people themselves, it is a weapon of the system."[9]

The family took all the necessities for their stay on the plantations—bedding, cooking utensils, and clothing. Sometimes employers paid them by the day and sometimes for the amount of work done. Children who did not work did not earn any pay and were not fed. The little ones who worked got a ration of tortillas. Rigoberta's mother had to share her ration of food with her.

The plantations had a cantina owned by the landowners that sold food, alcohol, and sweets. The children always pestered their parents for sweets, cakes and soft drinks. The prices were marked up on an account, and at the end of the work period when the workers were paid, they had to settle their debt, which was always a lot. For example, if a child accidentally broke a branch of a coffee bush, the worker had to work to make it up. Every plantation had a cantina where workers got drunk and piled up huge debts. They often spent most of their wages just paying off the debt. Rigoberta sadly remembered her father and mother going to the cantina out of despair. She commented, "But he hurt himself twice over because his money went back to the landowner. That's why they set up the cantina anyway."[10]

When Rigoberta turned eight she started to earn money on the plantation by picking coffee, and when the family returned to their mountain home, she worked in the fields growing maize (corn).The plantation work was very hard and her parents were usually exhausted. She noted that most of the women who worked picking cotton and coffee had 9 or 10 children. Of these, 3 or 4

were healthy and would survive, but most of them had swollen bellies from malnutrition and the mother knew that 4 or 5 of her children would die. Even Rigoberta's brother died from malnutrition. Men who had been in the army often abused young girls. Many girls had no families and turned to prostitution. She was sad to see this happen since prostitution did not exist in Indian culture.

Rigoberta celebrated her 10th birthday in the Altiplano. Her parents explained her responsibilities and that soon she would be a woman who could start having children. On her

Guatemalan ceremonies

12th birthday, it was the custom to receive a gift of a small animal to raise; her father gave her a pig. She sold weavings that she did in her spare time, after working in the fields all day, to get enough money to buy food for her pig.

The Indigenous Worldview

Rigoberta's community respected many things connected with the natural world. For example, water was sacred to her community. She explained, "Water is pure, clean, and gives life to humans. The same is true for the earth. The earth is mother of humans, because she gives us food. Her people eat maize, beans and vegetables; they cannot eat things made with equipment or machines. That is why they ask the earth's permission to sow maize and beans." Copa, the resin of a tree, was a sacred ingredient in candles for her people. The candles gave off a strong, smoky, delicious aroma when burned, and they were used in ceremonies to represent the earth, water and maize. They prayed to their ancestors and recited ancient prayers. Their grandfathers said they must ask the sun to shine on all its children: the trees, animals, water, man and enemies. To them, an enemy was someone who steals or goes into prostitution.

A happy moment in village life was when the farmers planted maize. They had a fiesta in which they asked the earth's permission to cultivate her. They lit candles and offered prayers and then blessed the seeds for sowing. According to the ritual, they honored the seed because they buried it in the sacred earth and by the next year it would multiply and bear fruit. They did the same with beans. When the maize started growing on their farms, they went back down to work on the plantations. When they came back, the maize had reached maturity. Maize was the center of their culture; they believed they were made of maize. They thanked mother earth for the harvest. After they harvested their crops, they all gathered together for a feast.

Every village had a community house where they all assembled to celebrate their faith, to pray, and to enjoy special ceremonies and fiestas. They all worked communally to clear bush in the mountains, and when sowing time came, the community met to discuss how to share the land, whether each one would have his own plot or if they would work it collectively. Everyone joined in the discussion. In her village, they decided to have their own plots of land but also to keep a common piece

Indigenous women

of land shared by the community. If anyone was ill or injured, s/he would have food to eat from the communal land. It mostly helped widows. Each day of the week, someone would work the communal land.

Rigoberta saw a stark difference between indigenous and modern education. To indigenous people, nature was their teacher. Her father was very suspicious of modern schools and said that once people learned to read and write, they weren't any use to the community anymore. They moved away and were indifferent toward their community. Rigoberta wanted to go to school to learn to read and write. Her father said she would have to learn on her own since he had no money for her education. He thought she was trying to leave the community and was concerned that she would forget her heritage. She still insisted she wanted to learn. Despite her father's misgivings, she sporadically attended a Catholic school.

As an adult, Rigoberta suffered a great deal at the hands of the government and military who wanted to suppress her work and exploit her fellow indigenous people. In response to the suffering she witnessed she dictated her autobiography, *I, Rigoberta Menchu* (1984), to telling the world not only about her own story but also about the lives of her fellow indigenous people. Her book and her social justice campaign brought international attention to the conflict between indigenous people and the military government of Guatemala. In 1992, she was awarded the Nobel Peace Prize and used the $1.2 million cash prize to set up a foundation to continue the fight for human rights of indigenous peoples. Due to her efforts, the United Nations declared 1993 the International Year for Indigenous Populations. Menchú now serves as a UNESCO Goodwill Ambassador and is a figure in indigenous political parties.

Questions to Consider

1. What inspiration do you feel we can gain from Rigoberta Menchu's story?
2. For those who are not inspired by her story, why not?

CONCLUDING INSIGHTS: THE INDIGENOUS WORLDVIEW

Indigenous peoples often have much in common with other neglected segments of societies, such as lack of political representation and participation, economic marginalization and poverty, lack of access to social services and discrimination. Despite their cultural differences, indigenous peoples share common problems related to the protection of their rights. They strive for recognition of their identities, their ways of life and their right to traditional lands, territories and natural resources.

Smiling friends, !Kung, Africa, photo Izla K. Bardavid

Indigenous peoples are the holders of unique languages, knowledge systems and beliefs and possess invaluable knowledge of practices for the sustainable management of natural resources. They have a special relation to their land and its traditional uses. Their ancestral lands have a fundamental importance for their collective physical and cultural survival. Indigenous peoples hold their own diverse concepts of development, based on their traditional values, visions, needs and priorities. They have much to teach us.

Questions to Consider

1. Do you feel that indigenous peoples have much to teach us? If so, what? If not, why not?

Since the modern worldview was introduced in contrast to the indigenous worldview, let's next turn to the modern worldview and look at it in more depth.

CHAPTER THREE

The Modern Worldview

"One of the most destructive things that's happening in modern society is that we are losing our sense of the bonds that bind people together - which can lead to nightmares of social collapse."

— Alexander McCall Smith

THE MODERN WORLDVIEW: AN INTRODUCTION

The modern worldview traces its historical origins back more than 500 years to the expansion of Western European power and its influence and ultimate dominance around the world. This view has been especially powerful over the last two centuries and has expanded to the farthest reaches of the world. **Modern** means relating to present and recent time and not ancient, remote, or obsolete. The modern worldview has ushered in a host of astonishing achievements such as the equality of women, medical breakthroughs, educational progress, and advancement of human rights, as well as appalling failures such as values of rampant consumerism, cut-throat competition, unlimited economic growth, the disintegration of community, military force to resolve conflict, and subjugation of nature. One of the challenges of the 21st century is how to draw on the achievements coming from a modern worldview and rethink or discard the darker elements.

We will start our examination of the modern worldview around the watershed date of 1500. It was at this time that a number of interrelated factors started the process of shaping a modern worldview: the Renaissance, European exploration, the unleashing of capitalism, the Scientific Revolution, and the Protestant Reformation. From these origins, the modern worldview evolved and morphed as different factors continued to shape its characteristics, ideology and traditions. As a result of the coalescing of these various factors, powerful forces emerged that sparked changes in the way of life for people in Western Europe

Modern Worldview

extols scientific reasoning
exalts individualism
promotes political liberalism
separates church and state
advances secularism
promotes consumerism
follows socialism or capitalism
places faith in technology
diminishes role of family
neglects community
commodifies nature
thinks chronologically and rationally
justifies conquest and domination

and then unevenly diffused at various times and places around the world. Of course, the introduction of a modern worldview around the world was not uniformly assimilated by those it encountered, but shaped by cultural differences, geography, and many other factors. Some people exposed to the modern worldview eagerly accepted the changes while others violently resisted it.

Let's look at the ideological, philosophical, scientific, religious, political, environmental and economic characteristics of the modern worldview in more depth.

MODERN THOUGHT

The European Renaissance ushered in changes in the European consciousness. Roughly encompassing the dates 1400-1600, a new spirit later called the Renaissance, swept across Europe among the educated, urban elite. Actually, there were two distinct Renaissances: first, a change in political, economic, social and religious conditions, and second, an artistic and cultural movement. The word **Renaissance** means "rebirth." The Renaissance, which began in Italy, was a renewal of Greco-Roman civilization. Above all, the Renaissance was an age of recovery from the disasters of 14th century Europe, such as the effects of the Black Death, political disorder, and economic recession. The Renaissance celebrated a new attitude. Now, the individual was extolled. A high regard for human dignity and worth and a realization of individual potentiality created a new social ideal of the well-rounded personality or universal person who was capable of achievements in many areas of life. Renaissance enthusiasts despised the Christian tradition of humility and encouraged a new pride in human improvement. A thirst for fame and a strong desire to put an individual's imprint upon the contemporary world were at the heart of the Renaissance.

Secularism and a focus on the here-and-now became the critical factor in determining acts and thoughts. The early Christian view of promoting a simple and humble way of life as it interpreted Jesus's life and teachings shifted to a view of life in which wealth and its acquisition were respectable. Few thought it wrong to pursue riches. Increasingly, people viewed life as an opportunity for glory and pleasure rather than as a transitory stage on the way to eternal bliss or everlasting damnation. Man was the measure of what life had to offer. The Renaissance also promoted new business techniques in banking, bookkeeping, trade, and commerce. Highly valued was the pursuit of profit, a departure from the Christian values of the Middle Ages. Unlike in earlier times, the merchant was elevated in status to reflect the growing impact of commerce. These Renaissance ideas would pave the way for further intellectual, scientific, political, economic and religious changes in the 16th century and beyond.

Michelangelo's David, symbol of the Renaissance

Fervent Protestant religious sects broke away from the all-powerful Catholic Church during the **Protestant Reformation**. Starting in 1517 with Martin Luther's break from the Catholic Church, these new religious sects set up their own denominations and celebrated religious beliefs that justified an emphasis on wealth acquisition. These new ideas, growing out of the Renaissance, accompanied the expansion and lure of a capitalist economic system. Protestants rejected the traditional Catholic beliefs, at least in theory, that saw poverty as akin to the life of Jesus. Instead, many Protestants, especially Calvinists, preached that material wealth was a favorable sign from God and should be embraced and not shunned. These new beliefs gave justification to the new attitude that wealth and its accumulation were respectable and in accord with Christian principles.

Around the 1500 time frame, the **Scientific Revolution** and the subsequent Enlightenment challenged the religious thinking of the time and instead celebrated the wonders of the scientific method and reason. The modern worldview is often called the Newtonian or mechanistic worldview since many of its characteristics are derived from how the famed English scientist Sir Isaac Newton (1643-1727) depicted the universe. He described the world as a giant machine operating in

a predictable, orderly mode; once the parts of the machine were individually analyzed, the whole machine could be explained. In Newton's universe, definable laws acted uniformly on objects that behaved predictably and consistently. Scientists busily set about classifying, dividing, and analyzing everything from plants and animals to human behavior. Nothing escaped their curious reach to scientifically examine and explain the planet.

Nineteenth century scientists continued their quest for scientific certainty. The French philosopher Auguste Comte postulated that all intellectual activity progressed through predictable stages: the theological or fictitious as the first stage, the metaphysical or abstract as the second stage, and the highest stage, the

Martin Luther, Protestant Reformation

scientific or positive. One of the most famous scientists of the modern age, **Charles Darwin** (1809-1882), theorized that humans were not divinely created, as the Christian world had confidentially assumed for centuries, but had evolved from simple to complex organisms through stages of natural selection.

The advancement of science contributed to the formation of the modern worldview. Scientific discoveries ushered in a change in values from religious values that were based on faith and miracles to scientific values based on evidence, reason, efficiency, rationality, orderliness, and analysis. Although the vast majority of Europeans, including many scientists, held to their religious faith during the Scientific Revolution, religious beliefs were starting to be devalued as unscientific, irrational and superstitious.

Questions to Consider

1. Do you think that the development of modern thought reflects holistic principles?

THE MODERN ECONOMY

European exploration or exploitation (depending upon your point of view), particularly of the Western hemisphere, contributed to the formation of a modern worldview. The Renaissance era of excitement and possibilities translated into more explorations by famed early explorers, such as Bartolemeo Diaz, Christopher Columbus, Amerigo Vespuci, Ferdinand Magellan, Francis Drake, Hernán Cortés, and many others. The reasons for propelling Western Europe in an explosion of outward exploration are significant in shaping the modern worldview. One of the reasons for this outward thrust of exploration was the relative poverty of Western Europe at the time compared to other regions of the world, especially Asia and the Middle East. Their material poverty stimulated expansion by their only option: the sea. The Europeans imported more goods from Asia than they exported to them; therefore, they had a trade imbalance that needed to be remedied. More gold and silver was flowing

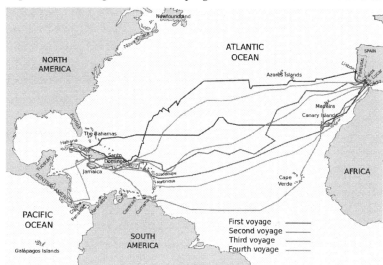

Columbus' voyages to the Western hemisphere

to Asia from Europe than coming in. Asians were quite self-sufficient and did not want or need any of the poor quality goods made by Europeans. But Europeans coveted China's luxury imports and spices from Southeast Asia. Exploration also signaled prestige, glory, and strength, attributes that Western Europeans craved. Hence, they invented or adapted from others technologically sophisticated weaponry and came to be known as "gunpowder empires." Their new technological inventions gave the West an edge in killing and intimidating around the world.

Accompanying the explosion of Western exploration was the expansion of a capitalist economic system. Wealth poured into Western European banks in cities like London and Amsterdam from the production of cash crops, such as sugar, tobacco, and cotton, as well as the fur trade and the mining of silver and gold. African slaves, indigenous peoples, and indentured servants provided cheap and coerced labor necessary for conversion of these raw materials into valuable commodities traded on the world market. An emerging middle class or *bourgeoisie* of bankers, merchants, financiers, and entrepreneurs capitalized on securing this new-found wealth for themselves. They acquired a taste for sugar, furs and many other luxury products that spurred a consumeristic frenzy. With the modern worldview, two main economic forms developed: capitalism (managed and free trade) and socialism/communism. Let's look at the two systems and the variations in each of the systems.

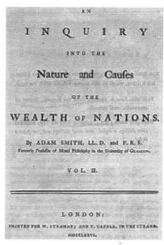

Adam Smith's capitalism manifesto

In a **capitalist** system private parties make their goods and services available in an open market and seek to make a profit on their activities. Private parties own the means of production. There are two variations of capitalism: free market capitalism, often called *laissez faire*, and managed or regulated capitalism. **Adam Smith** (1723-1790) is credited as the founder of free market economics, in which the "invisible hand" of the open marketplace would set prices according to the principles of supply and demand. This economic thinking emerged out of the liberal political traditions discussed below. Generally, Smith and free market capitalists are against the government's interference in the marketplace and argue that property should be privately or individually owned. They believe that tariffs (taxes on imported goods) should be eliminated in order to foster efficiency and competition in trade. Managed or regulated capitalism came about with the Great Depression in the 1930s and continued into the 1970s in the U.S. and other European countries. Supporters say that government should play an active role in regulating the economy in order for wealth to be somewhat equally distributed to a greater number of people than free market capitalism, in which wealth tends to concentrate in the hands of the wealthy.

Under managed capitalism, the government erects protective tariffs to shield national or local industries from cheaper competition abroad. For example, the United States, until recently, had protective tariffs on steel imported from other countries in order for the U.S. to have a profitable steel industry that provided jobs for thousands of U.S. workers. If the tariff was added to imported steel, say from low-wage China, that steel would be priced higher than steel made in the U.S. Therefore, the industries manufacturing such things as cars and appliances would pay a bit more for the steel used in production than if there were no tariffs. Of course, there are always many sides to any issue. Continuing with our steel example, with protective tariffs the price of goods manufactured in the U.S. would be slightly higher than if "free trade" (no tariffs) were allowed but, on the other hand, there are more workers employed in well-paid jobs in the U.S. to make the products using U.S. steel. In the U.S., the managed version of capitalism prevailed from the 1930s into the 1970s.

In 1980, the U.S. economic policy shifted to a version of capitalism called **laissez faire** capitalism, also called **neoliberalism** or free market capitalism. In this version of capitalism, government regulations and tariffs were lifted. The result has been lower prices for imported goods in the U.S., since many of products are now made in China, which has a lower cost of labor and production. But it has also resulted in a decline in the number of well-paid American manufacturing jobs, since many of these jobs have gone to nations where labor costs are low.

Nineteenth century scientists and social scientists continued the Enlightenment quest for scientific certainty. **Karl Marx**, (1818-1882), an early economic theorist, reasoned that human history advanced through stages of development from a feudalistic past, to the middle stage of capitalism, and then finally on to the pinnacle of human achievement: communism. Under a communist

economic system, also called a command economy, there is no private ownership. Instead of private ownership, the state collectively owns property for all. In theory, this economic form would avoid the exploitation of the common person by the wealthy elite who have amassed wealth in a capitalist system. The communist system was used in the Soviet Union in 1917 and continued for over 70 years, but in the end it failed miserably. Instead of a capitalist wealthy elite, a communist wealthy elite emerged who had power in the government and controlled the collective property of the citizenry. **Socialism** is an economic system in which the government owns and operates large industries such as military, education, transportation, health care, utilities and others, while small businesses are privately owned

Karl Marx

and operated and citizens can own private property.

It is interesting to place the different economic systems on a continuum where the differences of each system become apparent. Communism is considered on the far left of the continuum, while *laissez faire*, free market capitalism (neoliberalism) is considered to be on the far right. Socialism is placed to the immediate left of center, while managed capitalism is place to the immediate right of center. Many different economies around the world generally fall at some point on this continuum.

> ### Questions to Consider
> 1. Do you think the concept of capitalism is a product of modern worldview thinking? Communism? Socialism? Why or why not?

MODERN POLITICAL CHANGES

The Enlightenment of the 17th and 18th centuries was an intellectual movement that created the concept of political liberalism, celebrated the wonders of the scientific method and reason, challenged the religious thinking of the time, extolled the dignity of the individual, and defied the notion of absolute political authority. The Enlightenment *philosophes* argued for rational, written constitutions to limit the monarch's power and to ensure certain individual rights and equality before the law. They revered, above all else, reason, progress, objective thinking, and the optimistic idea that humans could be perfected through state-sponsored education and a rational society. Some *philosophes*, such as John Locke, advanced the merits of private property and the improvement of that property for monetary gain. The *philosophes'* ideas were particularly popular among the rising Western middle class who profited from their ideas, especially the concept of private property.

The Enlightenment *philosophes* posited the concept of political **liberalism** and defied the notion of absolute authority by either the church or monarchs. As a result of the political ideas of the Enlightenment, by the 19th century many countries in Western Europe and the United States had adopted some form of representative government guided by a written constitution. Although these were not direct democracies, this was a marked change from the days of absolute monarchical rule. Those represented in government expanded over the years from the common man—as long as he was male, white, over 21, and a property holder—to all individuals over the age of maturity (18 in the U.S.). With this move to a more inclusive political system, the idea of freedom and liberty for the individual, in the political sense, emerged. The idea of individualism and human rights became a new political value.

Another modern political change was the reconfiguration of political rule. For thousands of years, people lived in large empires, small states or city-states, or in decentralized territories ruled by feudal lords. With the modern worldview, there was a shift from those kinds of political rule to the **nation-state** as the preferred political structure. Great Britain, the United States, and later France pioneered the new political entity called the nation state, which became the accepted government structure. As new nation-states were formed in the 19th

John Locke, Enlightenment philosophe

and 20th centuries, the question remained: what kind of government would these new nation states embrace?

As mentioned above, the liberal form of government, (not to be confused with the liberal/ conservative division in the U.S. today) which advanced written constitutions and representative government, was adopted as a preferred form of political structure by many nations. But not all nation states in the modern era developed a liberal, representative type of government. Some nations have clung to the monarchy as a form of political rule; some have ceremonial monarchs, such as in the United Kingdom, and others have active monarchs such as in Saudi Arabia, Jordan, Morocco, and Kuwait.

Some nations turned to authoritarian types of government, most dramatically in the 20th century. For simplicity's purpose there are three main types of authoritarian rule found in the modern era: communism, fascism, and dictatorships. The values held by authoritarian regimes are obedience to authority, protection of the "mother land," strong masculine images, and patriarchal attitudes. Men defend the family against outside aggression, while women remain in the home raising the children. Honor, resolve, courage, valor, obedience, and vindictiveness are commonly held values.

Fascist dictators Hitler and Mussolini

The first form of authoritarian rule is **communism**, a theory or system of social organization based on the holding of all property in common with actual ownership held by the state. The Soviet Union, the first communist nation, was formed in 1917, when a revolution led by Vladimir Lenin overthrew the Russian monarchy. The Soviet Union continued as a communist form of government until its collapse in 1991. Pockets of communist rule still exist around the world, although mostly in a hybrid form in China, Cuba, Vietnam and North Korea. **Fascism**, the second form of authoritarian rule, is a radical and authoritarian nationalist political ideology. Germany (Nazis), Italy, and Japan were fascist governments leading up to and during World War II. The

Characteristics of Authoritarian Regimes

reject democracy

concentrate power among the elites

manipulate masses with untrue propaganda

stifle free press

cloak elite rule in secrecy

use fear to gain control and justify authority

propagate fear of outsiders

justify revenge against a threat or perceived threat

promote military images

wage constant war

portray life as a never ending struggle

value weaponry and the military above all

defend way of life against "perceived" outside aggressor

use warfare as a way to solve problems

employ excessive punishment and torture

blame others for problems

third form of authoritarian rule is a dictatorship, which is often established through a military coup after which the government is ruled by an individual dictator. Dictatorships have been common throughout the 20th century but are now outnumbered by republican forms of government.

The 20th century witnessed the darker side of the modern worldview. Two horrific world wars, fought over national competition, colonial acquisitions, and the struggle for world supremacy, exalted armed conflict as the preferred method for resolving differences. The Soviet Union and the United States challenged each other's ideologies in a Cold War (1945-1991). Although the two nations never came to blows, numerous proxy wars were fought, such as in Korea, Nicaragua, Vietnam, Afghanistan, and others. Although still severe, these Cold War battles were smaller in scope and brutality than World War II, perhaps reflecting the unspoken acknowledgment that our planet cannot survive the nuclear, environmental, and human devastation of another world war.

Even though the lessons of the two wars are readily apparent, some people today still cling to an authoritarian stance reminiscent of the oppressive rule imposed by many empires of the past, and the totalitarian regimes of the 20th century. Forms of authoritarian rule—dictatorships, monarchies, neo-fascist movements, militia groups, and communist rule—continue to survive, while pockets of militia groups' activity are found in parts of Europe and the United States. Although a controversial addition, some people argue that large multi-national corporations, run by corporate oligarchies, are a form of authoritarian rule, since they extend their non-democratic reach into every corner of the world.

Questions to Consider

1. Do you think nation-states are a product of modern worldview thinking? Why or why not?
2. If you live in the U.S., do you see any similarities as to what is politically happening today—the conflict between liberalism (middle), socialism/communism (left), fascism (right), compared to the past?

THE ENVIRONMENT IN THE MODERN WORLDVIEW

"The big problem of our modern society is that we feel that we are separated from nature. But it's just the opposite. We are interrelated and our DNA is the same."

— Marina Abramovic

With the modern worldview, nature's bounty was given economic value and assigned a specific price. The market value of fertile farmland was relative to the number of crops it could produce. This economic thinking meant that nature was not seen as a sacred source of beauty, awe, inspiration and reverence but as a supplier of resources, an economic commodity. Although probably unintentionally, Westerners tampered with the world's ecosystem by introducing new species into colonial areas and by over-hunting, overgrazing, and deforesting vast areas, which reduced, altered or exterminated fellow species.

Environmental catastrophe is largely a result of seeing the environment through the modern worldview lens. Resources are extracted from what is seen as inanimate nature in a detached and mechanistic way. Nature is an object, separate and inferior to human extractors. Often environmental damage is not experienced immediately but at some time in the future, yet the unseen, long-term consequences are conveniently ignored or postponed to a vague future date. Nature's purpose in this worldview is to provide the materials necessary for "progress" to be achieved by human beings.

The now-extinct passenger pigeon

MODERN SOCIETY

The modern worldview profoundly changed society and family patterns. The section on a comparison of the indigenous and modern worldviews in chapter 2 briefly described some characteristics of a modern worldview. This section highlights changes that have occurred in middle class, modern families from the 19th century onward.

In many middle class homes in the 19th century, a small nuclear family became the expected norm. The economic role of the middle class family shifted from one centered on production to one focused primarily on consumption of material goods. Along with consumption, the modern family's responsibilities included reproduction, socializing children, fulfilling psychic and emotional needs, instilling societal values, providing affection to all family members, guiding children's personality development, and encouraging and guiding school and career decisions for children.[1] Although these middle class family functions did not necessarily apply to the working class, peasants, or the elite, the nuclear family decreased in size, children were accorded greater parental affection, incidence of divorce increased, women became more independent, and the family no longer served as the center of economic activity.

Modern middle class marriages shifted from an arranged economic or political alliance to one based on individual choice. Individual choice, sexual and psychological attraction, affection, and personal satisfaction became important criteria in selecting a spouse, and more emotional interaction between middle class men and women took place. Marriage was carried out primarily to fulfill personal desires for home and children and to enhance personal happiness. Western Europeans socially and legally disapproved of polygamy. **Monogamy**, the normative marriage form in the West, expressed democratic, egalitarian ideals in reaction to inequalities and hierarchies often found in polygamous marital societies.[2]

The middle class family encouraged affection. The importance of love as an ingredient in family life became an important modern value. The family served as a pleasurable nurturing center that provided an emotional bond among individuals and a reliable, comfortable refuge from outside strife. With fewer children, childrearing practices among the modern middle class began to change. Parents increasingly treated children with love and respect. This practice coincided with Enlightenment beliefs, which assumed children could improve and become responsible adults through hu-

mane and supportive treatment. Harsh discipline as a means of dealing with childhood transgressions declined, although it certainly was not eliminated. Instead, it was believed that children should be afforded certain rights and protective services, and the tradition in which children were obliged to accept arbitrary parental directives decreased. Middle class parents spanked children less often and drew them more closely into the family orbit of affection. The old European practice of swaddling—wrapping infants tightly in cloth to prevent movement—began to disappear. Adult supervision

19th century European middle class family

increasingly replaced physically restraining children.[3]

Parents experienced a decline in their traditional authority, especially the father's role as authoritative head of the family. Although the father's influence did not fade away completely, this subtle decline of traditional family authority and male preeminence were linked to a lessening of family members' reliance upon each other for mutual benefit and even survival. Instead, family dependency shifted towards more reliance on the outside marketplace as a source of necessities and income. In middle class families, the fathers, some mothers, and children spent at least parts of the day outside the home, which meant that at least a partial transfer of family influence shifted to other institutions, such as schools or the workplace, which began to take over some of the family's traditional functions.[4]

Through the years, many people holding a modern worldview have fought for steady, incremental progress in forging a more equitable and inclusive society. Supporters of various **social movements**—civil rights, feminism, Native American rights, environmental protection, LGBT rights, people with disabilities, and others—have supported the recognition and implementation of legal, political,

Civil Rights march in the 1960s

and other rights that have helped those discriminated against win greater inclusion into mainstream society. Although the results have been uneven, blatant discrimination of minorities has been tempered and society, especially among the younger generation, is now more accepting of diversity than previous generations.

POST-MODERNISM

During the 20th century, there have been influential movements that have critiqued and even rejected the modern worldview. Since the modern worldview was and continues to be so pervasive and influential, another worldview has not stepped in to claim the dominant spot. But the unraveling of the modern worldview continues to provide space for the emergence of other worldviews and movements, as we will see in the next chapters on fundamentalist, globalized, and transformative worldviews. However, one movement, post-modernism, is worthy of examination to show the process of the diminishing and undermining of the modern worldview.

Post-modern literally means after the modernist movement, but it is generally seen as a point of departure from or a rejection of the modern worldview. The post-modern perspective in the late 20th and early 21st centuries has largely been used in works of literature, drama, architecture, cinema, journalism and design, as well as in marketing and business and in the interpretation of history, law, culture and religion. I think it is useful to discuss the post-modern movement at this point in order to have a clearer idea of the modern worldview.

Post-modernism can be traced to the Romantic poets and authors of the early 19th century. Poets such as William Wordsworth and Samuel Coleridge rejected what they regarded as the Enlightenment's stifling adoration of reason and instead emphasized passion, emotion, intuitive ways of knowing and the beauty of nature in their works.

Albert Einstein

Another contribution to post-modern thought came from the early 20th century physicists, who challenged the rational, objective modern worldview and the mechanistic order outlined by Newton. The **theory of relativity**, formulated by **Albert Einstein** (1879-1955) in 1905, shattered Newtonian certainties and introduced the element of uncertainty: time and space are relative to the viewpoint of the observer and only the speed of light is constant for all frames of reference in the universe. Max Planck proposed that the energy released by atomic particles did not flow smoothly but jumped in discontinuous spurts or quanta, leading to the formulation of quantum theory. Scientists also concluded that both wave and particle theories, although seemingly contradictory, coexisted logically—hence, the theory of complementarity. Instead of Newton's dependable, rational laws, there seemed to be only tendencies and probabilities, and scientists could never attain more than probable knowledge and certainty was impossible.

Equally unsettling as advances in physics were developments in psychology that disputed traditional, Victorian concepts of morals and values. According to Sigmund Freud (1856-1939), human behavior was basically irrational; the primitive unconscious was driven by sexual aggression and pleasure-seeking desires. Human behavior was a delicate and unpredictable compromise between instinctual drives and the controls of rational thinking and moral values.

Twentieth century novelists responded to Freud's irrational interpretation of the human mind by using a stream-of-consciousness technique to explore the psyche. Virginia Woolf's novel, *Jacob's Room*, consisted of a series of internal monologues, in which ideas and emotions from different periods of time randomly bubbled up. In James Joyce's novel *Ulysses*, published in 1922, conventional grammar was abandoned and replaced by a bewildering confusion of language intended to mirror modern life: a colossal riddle waiting to be unraveled. In his famous poem *The Waste Land* (1922), T. S. Eliot depicted a world of growing desolation and despair.

Post-modernism in the artistic realm included post-impressionist painters. They desired to know and depict an unseen, inner world of feeling and imagination, expressing an obscure psychological view of reality as well as evoking powerful emotions. Vincent van Gogh painted the vision of his mind's eye in *The Starry Night* (1889) with blazing trees and exploding stars all swirling together in one great rhythmic cosmic dance. Pablo Picasso founded the cubist movement which depicted a complex geometry of zigzagging lines and abstract sharply angled planes. And Wassily Kandinsky turned away from nature and painted form and color which represented mood and emotion, not representation of objects as in modern paintings.

British author and feminist, Virginia Woolf

Jazz, a postmodern musical expression of African Americans, diverged sharply from the classical tradition. Played by bands, in contrast to the highly organized symphony orchestra representative of

Vincent Van Gogh's Starry Night

the modern worldview, jazz was improvisational, and the lead performer often spontaneously invented and varied both melody and rhythm in non-standard repetitions. Dance experienced a similar break from tradition. Classical ballet dancers, a representation of the modern worldview, performed on a separate stage from the audience in a remote and detached manner. In contrast, modern dancers broke from the rituals of ballet and spontaneously conveyed their individual and deeply personal emotions and passion. In jazz clubs and cabarets, dancers energetically merged into the emotional ecstasy of the music and were not detached, remote performers.

Postmodern cultural thought continued in the 1970s, and by the beginning of the 1980s was well placed in the intellectual community. During the 1970s and 1980s, according to many post-modern thinkers, tremendous technological innovations in computer technology and communication devices rendered the individual mind servant to "artificial intelligence." Individual accomplishment, effort, and identity were dwarfed and often felt obliterated by the spread of technological advances. Influenced by these developments, postmodern thought has a quality of arbitrariness, randomness, a lack of restraint, and the propensity for diverse cultural strains and theories.[5] Postmodern culture is a fragmented world of sub-cultures and small groups and has no integrating cultural theory.

Early computer

42

Deconstruction is the name of an approach (whether in philosophy, literary analysis, or in other fields) which pursues the careful reading of a text. It embraces self-referentiality, which regards the text as a self-enclosed, structural world of knowledge. Deconstructionists advance the idea of conflictuality, which means that within texts there are internal conflicts at work, while the process of deconstructing the text includes taking the surface meaning of the text and breaking it down. The text disintegrates because of the oppositional and conflictual nature of language, breaking itself down into several layers of meaning. According to deconstructionists, there are infinite meanings in texts, moving from the conscious layer toward the unconscious. Anomalies or gaps exist on the surface of the text that represent the conflict between words and meaning. As one focuses on these gaps, the text begins to deconstruct itself. It is not the critic who deconstructs the text but the text deconstructs itself—the observer and observed are one.[6]

Deconstructionists reject the liberal, modern, humanist tradition, which emphasizes fixed meanings, a set canon of scholarly works, tradition, hierarchy, and objectivity. Instead they see only infinity of meaning. This deconstructionist theory erodes classical, rational liberalism, the cornerstone of the modern worldview.

The audience for post-modernism has been limited mostly to academics. Despite its opaque message, the impact of post-modernism has trickled down to the masses and influenced mainstream or mass culture. For example, the narrative in television dramas is often fragmented, does not follow sequential order, and does not offer a clear message.

Key Descriptors of Post-Modernism

autonomous, discontinuity
randomness, uncertainty
tendency, irrationality
bleakness, pessimism
unpredictability
relativity, abstract
lack of sequence
self-reference, connections
specialization, diversity
approximations
differentiation, subjectivity
rejection of tradition

Questions to Consider

1. Do you think people have given up on post-modernism? Why or why not?
2. Can you give examples of how post-modernism has trickled down to mass culture?

CONCLUDING INSIGHTS: THE MODERN WORLDVIEW

Many individuals continue to follow a modern worldview with its accompanying values of rampant consumerism, cut-throat competition, unlimited economic growth, faith in technological progress, secularism and criticism of religion, use of force as a way to resolve problems, punishment as a way to correct behaviors, unwavering patriotism and the staunch defense of individualism. The modern way of understanding the world and solving problems continues today in countless ways. For example, the decision to invade Iraq in 2003 was made, I contend, through a modern worldview lens. Based on an optimistic scenario in which the people of Iraq would gladly welcome conquering American troops, Iraqi

Invasion of Iraq, 2003, Baghdad

43

progress would be achieved through the introduction of democratic institutions and policies in a predictable, rational manner. The certainty that Iraqis would enthusiastically embrace American-style democracy and capitalism was detached from the reality of the situation.

Questions to Consider

1. Do you feel that the creative forces outweigh the destructive forces in the modern worldview, or vice versa? Explain.

Although the modern worldview continues to be fervently held by many people, it is not the only worldview at the present time. In this time of tumultuous change, other worldviews have developed that have grown out of or even reject the modern worldview and established their own distinct, coherent worldviews. Let's turn next to the fundamentalist worldview.

CHAPTER FOUR

The Fundamentalist Worldview

"At its most basic, the allure of fundamentalism, whether religious or ideological, liberal or conservative, is that it provides an appealing order to things that are actually disorderly."

— *Peter Mountford*

AN INTRODUCTION TO FUNDAMENTALISM

A new form of religiosity, popularly known as fundamentalism, is part of the post-modern rejection of modernity that was described in chapter 3. I will use the term fundamentalism in this chapter to describe a group of people who embrace this worldview. **Fundamentalism** refers to a belief in a strict obedience to a set of basic principles, often religious in nature, which is a reaction to perceived compromises with modern social, ideological and political life.[1] Although many fundamentalists resent having a Christian term imposed on their religious movements—nonetheless, this is a commonly used term and I will use it in this chapter to refer to a widespread worldview and a complex phenomenon. Many fundamentalists have strong opinions about social, economic and political issues and some voice their opinions in a forceful and sometimes violent manner.

Fundamentalism has largely retained its religious references, but the term has more recently been generalized to mean strong obedience to any set of beliefs in the face of criticism or unpopularity.

A niqab, head covering

Some writers refer to any literal-minded philosophy with the pretense of being the sole source of objective truth as fundamentalist, regardless of whether it is called a religion. For example, some people hold the belief—called market fundamentalism—that market capitalism is best and can correct all of society's ills. Extreme fundamentalists in the U.S. who have assassinated several abortion doctors believe their act of murder is justified to save the life of the unborn. On the other hand, in France, the imposition of restrictions on public display of religion has been labeled by some as "secular fundamentalism." French officials have proposed a bill that would ban women from wearing a head scarf in public, a policy directed towards Muslim women who wear a head covering as part of their religious tradition.[2] The application of the term fundamentalist to both religious and social-political approaches and actions, in my estimation, seems appropriate. However, in this chapter, I will primarily concentrate on religious fundamentalists, since this group seems to the most vocal and forceful.

Religious fundamentalism is a rejection of and reaction to the modern concepts of secularism and humanism. The shift to secular and humanistic beliefs started during the Enlightenment era of the 18th century and intensified in the 20th century. **Secularism** is the concept that government or other entities should exist separately from religion and/or religious beliefs. For example, the separation of church and state is a secular belief. **Humanism** attaches importance to human dignity, concerns, and capabilities, and particularly to reason. It emphasizes humanity more than the religious and rejects the supernatural or magical elements of religion. In the 21st century humanists tend to strongly endorse human rights, including reproductive rights, gender equality, social justice, and the separation of church and state. Secularists and humanists have often attacked religious doctrines as scientifically unproven and incompatible with scientific principles. As a result, many fundamentalists feel assaulted by the secular and/or humanist movement and strive to stem the tide of its influence.

For religious fundamentalists, sacred scripture is considered the authentic and authoritative word of their religion's god or gods. Fundamentalist beliefs depend on the twin doctrines that their god or gods articulated their will clearly to prophets and that followers have an accurate and unfailing record of that revelation. Fundamentalists see their religion as true and others as false, usually resulting in a denouncement of alternative religious practices and interpretations. There are fundamentalist sects in almost all of the world's major religions: Christianity, Islam, Buddhism, Hinduism, Judaism and others. Across cultures, fundamentalism is characterized by a cluster of common characteristics including a literal interpretation of scripture, a suspicion of outsiders, a sense of alienation from the secular culture, a distrust of liberal elites, and belief in the historical

Buddhist fundamentalism, Sinhalese, Sri Lanka

accuracy of their own interpretation of their religious scriptures. Religious fundamentalists are often politically active, strive to shape the social order in line with their beliefs, and feel the state should be administered according to their religious principles.

Fundamentalism is a movement through which its followers attempt to rescue their religious identity from inclusion into modern, secular Western culture. They have created a separate identity based on their particular religious community and upon the fundamental or founding principles of their religion. This formation of a separate identity is deemed necessary as a defensive measure to stem the real and perceived assault from the modern world. Often they see the choices for the organization of their nation as limited to a modern society or a traditional society. Since they reject a modern society, the only other choice they see is the preservation of their traditional ways. Also, many people in modern nations find that traditional values give resolute comfort and reassurance in a fluctuating and inexplicable world. Therefore, many people from the Middle East, to India, to the United States find that the familiar traditions of the past give meaning, identity, and steadfastness

Ultra orthodox Jewish wedding

to their lives. Although the fundamentalist worldview is very diverse and not unchanged from the past, the essence of many of these beliefs continues today and is zealously held by millions, if not billions, of people throughout the world.

Many scholars see most forms of fundamentalism as having similar traits. In the United States, for example, a pattern of the conflict between fundamentalism and modernism in Protestant Christianity has parallels in other religious communities as well. This is especially obvious if the mainstream society, such as the U.S., holds modern, secular or even atheist values as the norm. The fundamentalist views are thus seen as minority views and relegated to an inferior status. Religious scholar Peter Huff wrote: "Fundamentalists in Judaism, Christianity, and Islam, despite their doctrinal and practical differences, are united by a common worldview which anchors all of life in the authority of the sacred and a shared ethos that expresses itself through outrage at the pace and extent of modern secularization."[3] Religious scholar Karen Armstrong has found that three forms of fundamentalism—Christian, Islam, and Jewish—nearly always begin as a defensive movement; it is usually a response to a campaign of coreligionists or fellow countrymen that is experienced as hostile and menacing.[4]

Fundamentalist beliefs are often thought to have a direct and unbroken connection with the past. Despite the centuries that have passed since the origins of these universal religions, the fundamentalists give the impression that their particular religious interpretation is the one that mostly closely reflects the intent of the religious founders. This is not true. The fundamentalist version of their particular religion, be it Christian or Muslim, grew out of a particular history. A brief history of three fundamentalist faiths—Christianity, Islam, and Judaism—gives a clearer understanding of how they have arrived at their present stance. I have not started the history at the beginning of the religious traditions; instead I have started the history with modernization. These fundamentalist traditions are a reaction to modernity rather than an exact replication of the religion of the past. I am assuming that most readers of this book are more familiar with the Christian tradition than other religions; therefore, I will devote more to its history than the other fundamentalist interpretations.

CHRISTIAN FUNDAMENTALISM

As many of our schoolbooks tell us, Europeans came to North America to escape religious persecution in their native lands. Catholics and Protestants—Puritans, Mennonites and Quakers—settled in the English colony with the guarantee to practice religious freedom. Although there were attempts

to establish a state-administered religion in some colonies, such as by the Puritans in the Massachusetts Bay Colony, by and large these attempts proved to be too cumbersome and were banned completely or were replaced with governments that practiced separation of church and state. The Enlightenment principle of separation of church and state took root in the newly formed United States. In fact, many of the founding fathers and elites, such as Thomas Jefferson, were deists. **Deists** believed that religious truth in general could be determined using reason and observation of the natural world alone, without needing faith or organized religion.

Puritans, early Christian fundamentalists

By the 1830s, Deism had been marginalized in the nation and a new version of **Evangelicalism** became very popular. Its objective was to convert believers to the good news of the Gospel. They wanted a religion of the heart, not the Deist's remote religion of the head. They wanted the faithful to follow biblical authority and to personally commit to Jesus. According to Evangelical ideas, faith did not require learned philosophers and scientific experts, as was the case with Enlightenment philosophers; it was a simple matter of felt conviction and virtuous living. From those on the frontier to the developing cities of the Northeast, they were ready to listen to a new kind of preacher who stirred up a wave of revivals known as the Second Great Awakening (1800-35).[5]

Evangelical Christianity led many Americans away from the levelheaded rationality of the

Age of Reason to the kind of anti-intellectualism and rugged individualism that still characterizes American culture. The leaders of the Second Great Awakening were not educated men, and their rough, populist, democratic Christianity seemed far removed from the Deism of the founding fathers. Preachers held torchlight marches and mass rallies, and the new practice of gospel singing elevated audiences to the point where they openly wept and shouted for joy. Like some of the fundamentalist

movements today, these congregations gave people who felt marginalized and exploited by the wealthy elites and mainstream society a means of making their voices head. They were mistrustful of learned experts; they wanted a plain-speaking religion with no impenetrable theological arguments.[6]

Unlike many fundamentalists today, Evangelicals saw religion as a firmly rational faith and in keeping with science. They believed that God could be known through science as a matter of common

Second Great Awakening

sense. To them, there was only one path to truth, so theology must follow the scientific method.[7] In line with their faith in science, fundamentalists read the scriptures with an unparalleled literalism, because this seemed more rational than the older way of seeing scripture as allegory. Like scientific language, they reasoned, religious language should be clear, transparent, and have only one meaning. The Evangelicals also brought the Enlightenment concept of "belief" to the center of Protestant fundamentalism. They followed the Enlightenment *philosophes* in making the practice of morality central to religion. They declared that humans were good in exactly the same way as God. Interestingly, they enthusiastically embraced the virtues of thrift, sobriety, self-discipline, diligence, and temperance that ensured success in the expanding capitalist marketplace.[8]

Like today, the Evangelicals of the 1820s threw themselves into moral crusades that fought

Charles Darwin

against slavery, urban poverty, exploitation, and liquor, and campaigned for penal reform, the education of the poor, and the emancipation of women. They celebrated the worth of each human being, egalitarianism, and the ideal of inalienable rights. Today, as in the 1820s, these causes are considered to be on the liberal end of the political spectrum but in the current climate fundamentalist trend toward conservative, political and social views. By the mid 1800s, perhaps as a result of the Evangelical initiative, Americans were more religious than ever before.[9]

In 1859 **Charles Darwin** (1802-1882) published his ground-breaking book *On the Origin of Species* in which he presented his scientific theory that all species of life have evolved over time from common ancestors, and this pattern of evolution resulted from a process that he called natural selection. At first most Christians did not appreciate the full implications of natural selection and accommodated the theory. During the late 19th century Darwin was not yet the monster that he would later become. In fact, Christians argued that God was at work in natural selection and that humanity was gradually evolving to a greater spiritual perfection.[10] They had not yet fully evaluated how Darwinism had undermined the theology on which their belief was based. Today we are accustomed to the tension between science and religion, but in the late 19th century, most religious people still respected science. Actually, the Evangelicals did not bash science, but the popularizers of Darwin went on the offensive in an antireligious battle. The real divide in the 1800s was between liberal and conservative Christians. Conservative Christians insisted on the literal truth and factual accuracy of the Bible and all its stories and statements. Liberal Christians, on the other hand, did not interpret the Bible literally and read it more as allegory and story, rather than categorical fact.[11]

In 1906, the first congregation of Pentecostals formed and rebelled against modern rationalism. **Pentecostalists** were reacting against the more conservative Christians who were trying to make their Bible-based religion entirely reasonable and scientific. According to religious scholar Karen

Pentacostal baptism, Azusa St. Revival, Los Angeles, California, USA

Armstrong, "They claimed to have experienced the Spirit in a tiny house in Los Angeles, convinced that it had descended upon them in the same way as upon Jesus' disciples on the Jewish festival of Pentecost, when the divine presence had manifested itself in tongues of fire and given the apostles the ability to speak in strange languages." At a Pentecostal service, men and women fell into trance states, were seen to levitate, and felt that their bodies were melting in inexpressible joy. Within four years, there were hundreds of Pentecostal groups all over the U.S., and the movement had spread to 50 other countries.[12] The dramatic increase of this type of faith indicated widespread rejection of the modern rational, scientific culture. It developed at a time when many people were beginning to have doubts about science and technology.

Others followed a different approach to religion. **A.C. Dixon**, one of the founding fathers of Protestant fundamentalism in the 1920s, said his faith depended upon "exact observation and correct thinking." Religious doctrines were not theological speculations but facts. These Evangelical Christians still sought the early modern ideal of absolute certainty based on scientific verification. They would also see their experiences—born-again conversions, faith healing, and strongly felt emotional convictions—as positive confirmation of their beliefs. This claim to rationalism indicates, perhaps, a hidden fear. With the horrific battles of World War I fresh in their minds, many people had apocalyptic fantasies from Revelations and believed that the scriptures told that the Last Days were close at hand. Many Christians were now swayed to believe that they were on the front line of an apocalyptic war against Satan. They also no longer saw Jesus as a loving savior but rather as the foremost conservative.[13] Armstrong states that "Every single fundamentalist movement that I have studied in Judaism, Christianity, and Islam is rooted in profound fear." She found that the first fundamentalist movement in modern times followed that pattern. Dixon and his colleagues were reacting to the widespread discontent following World War I. They were assailed by liberal Christians, and the fundamentalists retaliated. They distorted the traditions they were trying to defend by underscoring the certainty and literalism of biblical scripture. They seemed to be gaining the upper hand until a new movement set them back for a few decades.[14]

A.C. Dixon

In the 1920s the Democratic politician **William Jennings Bryan** (1860-1925) launched a crusade against the here-to-for uncontroversial teachings of evolution in schools and colleges. Almost alone, he put Darwinism at the forefront of the fundamentalist agenda. He quoted a suspicious study that claimed evolutionary theory had played a role in Germany's determination to declare war in 1914, which had propelled the collapse of morality and decent civilization. Although his ideas were naive and incorrect, people were beginning to be wary of science and he found an agreeable audience. His lecture, "The Menace of Darwinism," drew large crowds and got widespread media coverage. At this time, the fundamentalist movement was largely limited to the northern states, but southerners had become troubled about evolution. In response to this unease about science, legislators passed a law in several southern states prohibiting the teaching of evolution in the public schools. The disquiet about evolution erupted in a public frenzy when John Scopes, a young teacher in Dayton, Tennessee, confessed that he had broken this law and in July 1925 was brought to trial. The new American Civil Liberties Union (ACLU) sent a team of lawyers to defend him, headed by the rationalist campaigner Clarence Darrow. When Bryan agreed to speak in defense of the anti-evolution law, the trial ceased to be about civil liberties and became a contest between religion and science.[15]

Like many fundamentalist disputes, **the Scopes trial** was a clash between two opposing points of view. Both Darrow and Bryan represented core American values: Darrow stood for intellectual

Scopes trial

inquiry and Bryan for the rights of the ordinary folk, who were traditionally wary of learned experts, had no real knowledge of science, and felt that urbane elites were imposing their own values on small-town America. While Darrow argued brilliantly on the stand, Bryan was a disaster. At the end of the trial, Darrow emerged as the hero of clear rational thought, while Bryan was seen as a blundering, inept relic who was hopelessly out of touch with the modern world.[16] Yet, in the long run, Bryan made anti-evolution thought a keystone of fundamentalism beliefs that continues today.

The Fundamentalist Worldview

After the Scopes trial, fundamentalists lost much of their appeal during the Depression, World War II, and the optimistic period of the 1950s and 1960s, but they had not gone away. They had simply withdrawn defensively, as fundamentalists of other traditions would do in the future. In

a world that seemed antagonistic to religion, they created an enclave of the faithful, forming their own churches, broadcasting stations, publishing houses, schools, universities, and Bible colleges. By the late 1970s, when they had gained sufficient strength and confidence, the fundamentalists would return to public life, launching an offensive to transform the nation to their principles.[17]

During the time of retreat, the fundamentalists became more radical, harboring deep criticism of mainstream American culture.

Darrow (l) and Bryan (r) at the Scopes trial

History would show that when a fundamentalist movement is attacked, it almost always becomes more hardline, acrimonious, and extreme. Since fundamentalism is rooted in fear of extermination, its followers see any attacks as proof that the secular or liberal world is intent on the eradication of religion. Jewish and Muslim movements would also follow this pattern. As noted, before the Scopes trial Protestant fundamentalists fell on the left of the political spectrum, willing to work with socialists and liberals in the poverty areas of the nation's rapidly industrializing cities. After Scopes

there was a distinct swing to the far right, where they have remained. The mockery of the press during and after the Scopes trial reinforced, not undermined, their movement; the fundamentalists became even more provocative of their views. Before the Scopes trial, evolution had not been an important issue, but afterwards a steadfast biblical literalism became central to the fundamentalist mind-set and creation science became the trademark of the movement. It would become difficult to discuss the issue sensibly, because evolution was no longer about scientific findings but a symbol of the deeply felt fear that religion would be crushed under the modern views of mainstream society. Armstrong notes, "When attacking religion that seems obscurantist, critics must be aware that this assault is likely to make it more extreme."[18]

Political cartoon of the Scopes trial, Boston Globe, 1925

Protestant fundamentalism made inroads into public awareness when it opposed new scientific discoveries. Fundamentalists in other traditions have been concerned by different problems and are not fixated on "belief" in the same way. In a clear departure from mainstream or liberal Christian tradition, fundamentalists are convinced that their religious beliefs are a precise, ultimate expression of sacred truth and that every word of the Bible is literally true. They believe that miracles are an essential promise of true faith and that God will give the believer anything he asks for in prayer. If an individual's prayers are not answered, perhaps something is wrong with the individual. Fundamentalists crusade against the teaching of evolution in public schools, are staunchly patriotic but suspicious of democracy, see feminism as one of the great evils of the day, and fight against abortion and homosexuality. Some extremists have even murdered doctors and nurses who work in abortion clinics. Like evolution, abortion has become emblematic of the murderous evil of modern society. They are intolerant of other faiths, see Jews and Muslims as fated for hellfire, and some regard Buddhism, Hinduism, and Daoism as devil worshippers.[19]

THE EXPANSION OF WORLD FUNDAMENTALISM: THE 1970S

Those who advocated for a rational, secular, modern worldview spoke too hastily of the death of religion. This became apparent when a dramatic religious uprising occurred in the late 1970s. From 1978-1979, the Western world watched as an obscure ayatollah brought down the government of Shah Muhammad Reza Pahlavi (1919-1980) in Iran, which had seemed to be one of the most modern and stable nations in the Middle East. At the same time as governments applauded the peace initiative of President Anwar al Sadat of Egypt (1918-1981), observers noticed that young Egyptians were donning Islamic dress,

Khomeini, brought down the Iranian government

casting aside the trappings of modernity, and engaging in a seizure of university campuses in order to reclaim them for religion—in a way that was reminiscent of student rebellions during the 1960s. In the U.S., Jerry Falwell (1933-2007) established the Moral Majority in 1979, urging Protestant fundamentalists to get politically involved and to challenge any state or federal legislation that supported a "secular humanist" agenda. In Israel, fundamentalists proclaimed Israel to be a religious state.[20]

Religious extremism emerged in regions where a secular, Western-style government had separated religion and politics. Its cohorts were resolute in dragging God and/or religion from the sidelines of modern culture and back to center field. It echoed a widespread disenchantment with modern culture. People all over the world were demonstrating that they wanted to see religion more openly reflected in public life, despite the derision heaped upon them by intellectuals and politicians.

Despite their intense dislike and distrust for each other, fundamentalist movements around the world share commonalities. They are quick to denounce people whom they regard as the enemies of God. Because fundamentalists feel under attack, they are distrustful and unwilling to consider any alternative point of view; this is yet another expression of intolerance that is a part of modernity. They take a hard line on what they regard as social morality.

Some modernizers have loudly called for the abolition of religion and have railed against religion as the root of all problems; they have done so in the past and continue to do so. Fundamentalists' movements begin with what they perceive as a real attack by followers of liberal or mainstream religions or a secularist state, and more attacks simply make them more extreme. This was seen in the U.S. after media attacks in the wake of the Scopes trial; Jewish fundamentalism advanced after Hitler tried to exterminate European Jews and after the October War in 1973 when Arab armies launched a surprise attack against Israel.[21]

In their anxiety and fear, fundamentalists often distort the faith they are trying to preserve. They are convinced that they are fighting for God but they can be highly selective in their reading of scripture. As Armstrong notes, for example, "Protestant fundamentalists quote from the book of Revelation at length and are stirred by its violent end-time vision but rarely refer to the Sermon on the Mount, where Jesus tells his followers to love their enemies, to turn the other cheek, and not to judge others. Jewish fundamentalists cite extensively from the Deuteronomy sections of the Bible and seem to overlook the rabbis' command for charity. Muslim fundamentalists pointedly ignore the Qur'an's numerous calls for peace, tolerance, and forgiveness, and extremists quote its more hard line verses to defend violence."[22]

JEWISH FUNDAMENTALISM

Many forms of fundamentalism are essentially political. In Israel, a bellicose religious form of Zionism (which had initially been a defiant secular movement) rose to political prominence. **Zionism** is a religious form of extreme nationalism or ethnicity. It is a Jewish movement that arose in the late 19th century in response to growing anti-Semitism in Europe and focused its nationalistic fervor into the

Jews protesting Zionism

founding of a Jewish homeland in Palestine. Modern Zionism supports the continuation, at times violently, of the state of Israel. Most Zionists are fanatically for the state of Israel and look upon its army, political institutions, and every inch of the Holy Land as sacred; others are fervently opposed to the idea of a secular state. This political fundamentalism in Israel has inspired religious extremists to insist on the forcible expulsion of Arabs from what they claim is Israeli land. The ultra-Orthodox parties, which David Ben-Gurion (1886-1973), Israel's first prime minister, had assuredly predicted would fade away once Jewish people had their own secular state, gathered even more strength after the state was established in 1948. Jewish fundamentalists have established illegal settlements in the West Bank, land illegally occupied during and after the 1967 war. Their intention is to drive out Arab residents since they believe according to their religion that they are paving the way for the Messiah. Other fundamentalists throw stones at politically moderate Israelis who drive their cars on the holy Sabbath. In 1995, Yigal Amir, a religious Zionist, assassinated Prime Minister Yitzak Rabin for signing the Oslo Peace Accords with the Palestinians.[23]

ISLAMIC FUNDAMENTALISM

Islamic fundamentalism, like Jewish fundamentalism, is also political. Muslim fundamentalists see their own tradition as the only true faith. They have toppled governments, and some extremists have been guilty of terrorist atrocities. In Islam at the turn of the 20th century most Muslims, with exception of Iranian zealot Jamal al-Din al-Afghani (1838-1897), embraced the West and modernity. For example, leading religious leaders in Iran campaigned alongside secular intellectuals for representational government and constitutional rule. They were successful in 1906. It is important to highlight this early interest in modernity because today too many Westerners regard Islam as essentially fundamentalist, constantly addicted to violence and opposed to democracy and freedom.[24]

Islam was the last of the three monotheistic religions to develop a fundamentalist strain. It did not do so until the late 1960s, after the Arabs' catastrophic defeat by Israel in the Six-Day War of 1967. The Western ideologies of nationalism and socialism influenced the elites of Arab nations at this time but had little grassroots support and appeared to have failed to take hold. Religion seemed a way of returning to the precolonial roots of their culture and regaining a more genuine identity. Western foreign policy has also aggravated the rise of fundamentalism in the Middle East. The U.S. led a coup in 1953 that overthrew the popular and democratically elected Prime Minister Muhammad Mosaddeq (1882-1967) in Iran, which left the Iranian people with a sense of animosity, shame, betrayal, and weakness. The failure to find a political solution to the Palestinian situation has also helped to radicalize some Muslims in the Middle East. Western support for such rulers as Shah Pahlavi of Iran and Saddam Hussein of Iraq, who denied their people basic human rights, has also tainted the ideals of democracy that the West proudly proclaims, while, at the same time, inflicting dictatorships on others.[25]

The hurried secularization and modernization of some of these Middle Eastern countries has often taken the form of an attack on religion. In Europe and the U.S. secularism gradually took place over a long period, and the

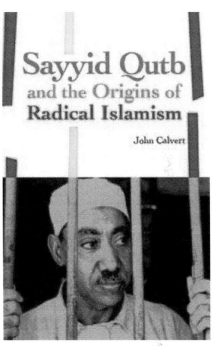

Sayyid Qutb imprisoned by secular President Nasser

new ideas and institutions had time to trickle down to all members of the population. But many Muslim countries had to rapidly adopt the Western, modern model in just 50 years or so. For example, the Shah of Iran made his soldiers go through the streets tearing off women's veils with their bayonets and ripping them to pieces. These reformers wanted their countries to look modern, even though only a small elite was familiar with Western principles. In 1935, Shah Pahlavi ordered his soldiers to shoot at a crowd of defenseless demonstrators who were peacefully protesting against compulsory Western dress in Mashhad, one of the holiest cities in Iran. Hundreds of Iranians died that day. When such events occur, secularism does not appear as a beneficial alternative.[26]

Sunni fundamentalism developed in the concentration camps in which President Gamal Abdel Nasser (1918-1970) held thousands of Muslim Brotherhood members without trial. Many of them had just handed out leaflets or attended a meeting. In these abominable prisons they were subjected to mental and physical torture and became radicalized. **Sayyid Qutb** (1906-1966) entered the prisons as a moderate, but after repeated torture and finally execution he evolved a radical ideology that is still popular among Muslims today. He was appalled with secularism when he heard Nasser vowing to confine Islam to the private sphere. In his writings, his paranoid vision of a group pushed too far became clear: Jews, Christians, communists, capitalists, and imperialists were all in league against Islam. He preached that Muslims had a duty to fight against the savagery of their day, starting with so-called Muslim rulers like Nasser.[27] In shifting the understanding of jihad from a personal struggle to be a good person according to the Kor'an to armed conflict, Qutb had distorted the faith that he was trying to defend. But he was not the first to do so.

The writings of Pakistani journalist and politician Abu Ala Mawdudi (1903-1979) influenced Qutb and other budding radicals. Mawdudi resented the effects of Western imperialism in the Muslim world, and in order to survive he believed Muslims must prepare for revolutionary struggle or jihad. He argued that this jihad could take many forms: some would write, others would engage in politics, but in the last resort Muslims must be prepared for war. No major Muslim thinker had ever made holy war a central tenet of the faith before; Mawdudi was convinced that this radical innovation was justified by the present political emergency. His aim was that toleration would be possible only after the political victory of Islam and the establishment of a truly Muslim community or *ummah*.[28]

Iraqi insurgents

The Palestinian party **Hamas** began as a resistance movement and started only after the secular policies of Yassir Arafat and his party, Fatah, appeared to have become both ineffective and corrupt. Hamas is not attempting to force the entire world to submit to Islam, has no global outreach, and targets only Israelis. Because any military occupation is likely to breed resistance, and since the Israeli occupation has lasted almost 50 years, this resistance is likely to take a violent form. However, the cult of murderous martyrdom is not widespread in the religion of Islam.[29]

In the Muslim world, the political state of the *ummah* has become vulnerable. The Qur'an insists that the primary duty of a Muslim is to forge a just and decent society, so when Muslims see the *ummah* exploited or even terrorized by foreign powers and governed by corrupt rules, they can feel as religiously offended as a Protestant who sees the Bible spat upon. The Qur'an assures them that if their society is just and egalitarian it will flourish because this type of government is in line with Islam's fundamental laws. But Muslims have been able to make little headway against the secular West, and some have found this as threatening as Darwinism seems to fundamentalist Christians.[30]

CONCLUDING INSIGHTS: THE FUNDAMENTALIST WORLDVIEW

Even though it is usually thought that fundamentalists are set on returning their religion to its historic roots of the past, actually these movements are of the time and could not have taken place at any other time than our own. As mentioned above, fundamentalism can be seen as another post-modern rejection of modernity. They are not conservative; indeed many are anti-orthodox and regard the more conventional faithful as part of the problem. These movements have sprung up autonomously, and each has its own idea of religious belief. However, they bear commonalities and are similar to the pattern set by American Protestant fundamentalism, the earliest of these movements.

Armstrong explains, "All are initially defensive movements rooted in a profound fear of obliteration, which causes them to develop a mistrustful vision of the "enemy." They begin as intra-faith movements, and only at a secondary stage, if at all, do they direct their attention to a foreign foe."[31]

Fundamentalists often see the choices as to the organization of their nation as limited to a modern society or society based on the traditions of an imaginary past. Since they reject a modern society, the only other choice they see is the preservation of their traditional ways. Also many people in modern nations find that traditional values give resolute comfort and reassurance in a fluctuating and inexplicable world. Therefore, many people from the Middle East to India to the United States find that the familiar traditions of the past give meaning, identity, and steadfastness to their lives. The essence of many of these traditional beliefs continues today and is zealously held by millions, if not billions, of people throughout the world.

Is this the new fundamentalism?

Fundamentalists fear modernity and the disrupting influences of globalization and know that some adversaries vow to destroy religion. They have found that their religion has provided them the sole guarantee of certainty in an increasingly uncertain and complex world. They will fight to their death to defend this certainty.

We next turn next to another worldview that has grown out of the modern worldview but has significantly morphed into its own worldview: The globalized worldview.

CHAPTER FIVE

The Globalized Worldview

"Globalization is not a monolithic force but an evolving set of consequences - some good, some bad and some unintended. It is the new reality."

— John B. Larson

INTRODUCTION: A GLOBALIZED WORLDVIEW

A fourth worldview, the globalized worldview, is sweeping the world today. A globalized worldview has greatly changed the landscape in which people around the world work, play, interact, and live their everyday lives. Greatly intensifying since the 1980s, it reflects the many ways in which people on an increasingly populated planet have been drawn together, not only by their own movements but also through the flow of goods, services, capital, labor, technology, ideas, and information. **Globalization** is a complex, multi-dimensional phenomenon that interconnects worldwide economic, political, cultural, social, environmental, and technological forces, while transcending national boundaries. It refers to the worldwide compression of space and time and the reduced importance of the nation-state. Through globalization the world has become a single place that serves as a frame of reference, influencing the way billions of people around the world conduct their everyday lives.

Descriptors of a Globalized Worldview

interconnections
blurring of boundaries
approximation, speed
demassification, networks
diversity, differentiation
specialization, productivity
consolidation, mergers
acquisitions, and interdependence

A globalized worldview incorporates many of the attributes of the modern worldview but intensifies and quickens the pace for the growth and expansion of this way of discerning the world. Arguably, globalization is most heavily influenced by the United States and is especially prevalent in intensely industrialized areas of Canada, Europe, Japan, and Australia, yet reaches across the world into parts of China, India, Southeast Asia, Latin America, and parts of the Middle East and Africa as well.

At this point, I would argue, a globalized worldview is the most all-encompassing worldview and continues its unabated outward expansion and lure. It expands and deepens the capitalist economic practices that were launched in the modern era. For many people, following a globalized worldview has "opened up" the world in many positive ways—communication networks, especially the Internet, transportation linkages and travel opportunities, sophisticated technology, breakthrough medical discoveries, diverse entertainment options, and comfortable living standards—but for others, the destructive effects of globalization have resulted in job loss, pension reductions, a loss of community and family, social isolation, depression and hopelessness, and a debasing of values, standards, and moral conduct. There are many other people who challenge its corporate dominance, unbridled consumerism, expedient business climate, ravaged environment, and effects on the human psyche.

A GLOBALIZED ECONOMY

Global capitalism is the dominant economic system in the world, with almost all nations pulled into its economic web. National and local economies, regulated and protected by national and local governments, have been largely folded into one integrated economic system governed by capitalist principles. Business, currency exchanges, and trade policies are conducted in a global economic marketplace that ignores national boundaries. Global multinational corporations make many of the rules and conduct the business of the world marketplace. They promote a consumer-focused economy by extending their broad influence to the farthest reaches of the globe.

In the modern worldview capitalism and communism and their variants were the two dominant economic systems to guide the economies of modern nations. With the collapse of communism in the early 1990s, the American form of capitalism reigned. Even the former communist nations seemed to eagerly embrace capitalism. Today, the global economy can be separated into three related dimensions: neoliberalism/ state capitalism, economic globalization, and the financial sector. Let's start with an examination of neoliberalism and state capitalism.

Apple headquarters, Cupertino, California, USA

Neoliberalism, a version of capitalism, has prevailed in the U.S. since the early 1980s. It is one of the ways in which the rules of the global economy operate. Although the concept is the same, it is also known as free market capitalism, free trade capitalism, supply-side economics, laissez-faire capitalism, classical capitalism, corporate capitalism, market fundamentalism, or an Anglo-American version of capitalism. "Neo" in neoliberalism means new, since it is a newer version of the classical economic system found in the 19th and early 20th centuries pioneered by Britain. Neoliberalism favors free trade, privatization, minimal government intervention in business operations, and reduced public expenditure for social services. Neoliberals give several reasons for the support of the system: self-interest motivates humans, competitive behavior is more rational than cooperation, materialism is a measure of progress, markets allocate resources most efficiently, governments should only provide infrastructure and enforce property laws and contracts, and inequality results from individuals failing to adapt to the new economic reality.

Neoliberals favor **multinational corporations** (MNCs), with services in at least two countries,

World Bank headquarters, Washington D.C.

as a form of ownership of capital in the global economy. MNCs have maneuvered to gain access and authority over the international rule-making institutions like the World Bank, World Trade Organization (WTO) and International Monetary Fund (IMF). The World Bank loans money to nations to build large infrastructure projects, the WTO governs the rules of global trade, and the IMF fosters global monetary cooperation. At this time, the rules of these three institutions favor Western countries and MNCs. Because rules made by these institutions take precedence over national laws, national enterprises are obliged to comply with them or risk economic ruin. Thus, these global institutions have generally usurped oversight of corporations from national governments. For example, national laws passed by a nation's legislative branch can be in violation of rules passed by the WTO and are, thus, subservient to the WTO rules.

After the collapse of communism, it appeared that the neoliberal model was becoming a global favorite. But in the 2000s, another version of capitalism—state capitalism—emerged as an attractive alternative to neoliberalism for many countries as a way to structure their economy. In state capitalism government officials direct markets to create wealth as they see fit. This economic system is not merely the re-emergence of socialist central planning in a 21st century package, but it is a form of state-engineered capitalism particular to each government that practices it. Political scientist Ian Bremmer defines **state capitalism** as "a system in which the state plays the role of leading economic actor and uses markets primarily for political gain." State capitalist governments believe that public wealth, public investment, and public enterprise offer the surest path toward political stability and economic development.[1] For example, the royal family of Saudi Arabia invests the kingdom's massive oil wealth for lucrative returns. The Chinese government sends state-owned firms abroad in search of long-term access to oil, gas, metals, and minerals. China continues to have a communist form of government with many state-owned enterprises, while also following an export-oriented form of capitalism in which the government supports industries that export products to other countries. Among the world's leading state capitalist countries are China, with ties to the Chinese Communist Party; Saudi Arabia, with ties to the Saudi royal family; and Russia, with ties to the powerful current president, Vladimir Putin.[2]

A second dimension of the global economy is economic globalization. **Economic globalization** refers to the increasing expansion of capitalism around the world, integrating non-capitalist economies into a world economic system. Even though countries may have different versions of capitalism, they still participate in the world economy. With economic globalization, trade, investment, business, capital, financial flows, production, management, markets, labor movement (although somewhat restricted), information, competition, and technology are carried out across local and national boundaries, subsuming many national and local economies into one integrated economic system governed by capitalist principles. There is also a growing concentration of wealth and influence in multi-national corporations, huge financial institutions, and state-run enterprises. With economic globalization has come the absorption or systematic destruction of centuries-old local/domestic economies around the world.

Ten Pieces of the Economic Globalization Puzzle

1. Reduction of local economies
2. Economic growth
3. Consumerism
4. Rule-making institutions
5. Free trade
6. Privatization and commodification
7. Concentration of corporate and state enterprises
8. Specialization
9. Reduce labor's influence
10. Military hegemony

Certain factors are necessary for economic globalization to function. These 10 factors are pieced together into an economic globalization puzzle. All of the puzzle pieces make up the full picture of economic globalization (see *The Global Economy: Connecting the Roots of a Holistic System* for more information). Nations are persuaded, some say duped, into conforming to the rules of economic globalization with the threat that if they do not participate in the global marketplace, they will be left behind in economic development.

The **financial sector**, the third component of the global economy, encompasses a broad range of institutions that deal with the management of money. Among these are banks (commercial and investment), credit card companies, insurance companies, consumer finance companies, stock brokerages, investment funds, foreign exchange services, real estate, and others. Currently, the Industrial & Commercial Bank of China is the largest bank in the world. The U.S. government has closely regulated these businesses since the 1930s, but in the 1980s deregulation of the industry gained steam.

ICBC headquarters, Bejing, China

Financialization took off after the crisis of the 1970s because of technological advancements that made it easier and more efficient to devise financial products and because of deregulation of the industry. As a result, there was a rash of sophisticated speculative financial products such as derivatives that escaped governmental monitoring and regulation. The trading in speculative financial products was little more than gambling; hence, the name "casino economy." In fact, speculative finance boiled down to an effort to squeeze more "value" out of already created value, instead of creating new value.[3] In other words, the goal was not innovation to create new wealth, but to try to get more margins

or value out of existing products and services. During this time, instability has rocked the financial sector, skipping from one crisis to another. The government has had a hand in rescuing the financial sector with "bail-out" packages funded by taxpayers. Thus, there is an increased bifurcation between the hyperactive financial economy, known as Wall Street, and the stagnant real economy, known as Main Street. This is not an accidental development; the financial sector exploded precisely to make up for the stagnation owing to overproduction of the real economy.[4]

Six of the Ten Globalized Economy Puzzle Pieces

1. Consumer Capitalism

Capitalism needs constant new sources of wealth creation to expand and grow. Since the 1980s, the expansion of consumerism has been the underpinning of wealth creation in the U.S. and global economy. For example, private consumption expenditures make up about 70 percent of U.S. GDP. Goods and services not only are provided to satisfy common needs but also to secure identity and meaning. Consumption is powerfully shaped by forces such as advertising, cultural norms, social pressures, and psychological associations. Sociologist Madeline Levine criticized what she saw as a change in American culture in the post-war years—"a shift away from values of community, spirituality, and integrity, and toward competition, materialism and disconnection."[5]

Capitalism has been immensely successful at producing goods and services for about 20 percent of the world's population who can afford these products, yet the other 80 percent of the world's population cannot. This is one of the many paradoxes of capitalism. It is supremely efficient at producing goods and services, but is not proficient at distributing them to those in real need. In fact, capitalism has been too successful in producing goods and services. Thus, producers have sought ways to induce consumers to buy more—more than they need. Enter the advertising industry. The single goal of this industry is to create gimmicks and enticements to convince consumers to purchase more and more.

Major brands

2. Advertising

The advertising industry finds ways to stimulate new consumer needs and desires, creating a malaise among those whose only cure is to buy more. The traditional values of the Protestant ethic that have shaped the American value system since the country's founding include thrift, hard work and its rewards, long-term planning, rational behavior, stability, and adherence to rules and laws. The dilemma for advertisers is that a person with these values does not impulsively consume. The advertising industry figured out that it needed to change individual behaviors and values to those that are impulsive, irrational, self-centered, and reckless. It launched a brazen campaign to do so.[6]

Adults holding to a consumerist ethic are pawns to the advertising industry. The demands of the mobile global economy have severed their ties to their traditional community; instead, their sense of belonging and identity has shifted to brands of consumer products. The brands selected by an

individual or family indicate their particular income, class, and place. These branded identities are superficial veneers replacing traditional ethnic, cultural, and national identity. Corporate names such as Nike, emblazoned on T-shirts and athletic wear, for example, identify the values of the wearer while providing free advertising for the company. Although it appears that we freely choose these identities, in reality they are reflective of the permeation of the ubiquitous commercial culture into every aspect of our lives. Advertisers happily promote this brand identification among consumers because it cuts across national and ethnic boundaries to mold a true globalization of identity.[7]

3. Economic Growth

Through much of human history, having more comforts and surplus food has made human lives easier. As populations have grown, so have economies. Unlimited growth made sense decades ago when the human population of the world was relatively low and natural resources for human consumption appeared to be endless. In this "empty world" money and human labor were the limiting factors, while natural resources were abundant. In this context, there was no need to worry about environmental destruction and social disruptions, since they were assumed to be relatively small and ultimately solvable. It made sense to focus on growth of the economy as a primary means to improve human living standards.[8]

Economic growth is the process by which wealth increases over time as the economy adds new market value to goods and services. It is an essential component of capitalism, which must expand constantly to generate new wealth. Its drive to accumulate and its built-in tendency to expand distinguish capitalism from other economic systems. Innovative activity—which in other types of economies is optional—becomes mandatory under capitalism, a life-and-death matter for businesses. Through history, the creation of new technology proceeded at an even-handed pace, often requiring decades or even centuries to develop, but under capitalism time speeds up because, quite simply, time is money.

Promoting growth—achieving ever-greater economic wealth and prosperity—may be the most widely shared and forceful cause in the world today. Industrial societ-

Economic growth

ies regard growth as their "secular religion."[9] We now live in a world relatively full of humans and the infrastructure that we built. In this new world, human populations and labor supply are vast, while the natural resources to support human life are limited. There is a dawning recognition that the growth model eagerly adopted by modern countries is no longer working; that model is geared towards a time in the past that differs from the reality of today. All this is happening at the expense of our natural world, which is being battered by the demand to produce more products for human consumption and absorb its wastes.

Individuals support growth policies because they accept the commonly held notion that growth will give them and the next generation a better standard of living. Governments seek growth as a remedy for just about every imaginable problem. Economists believe growth to be essential for full employment, upward mobility, and technical achievements. Politicians encourage growth because it expands the economic pie, and they can postpone hard choices.[10] Growth, development, progress, advancement, gain, success, improvement, and prosperity are deeply embedded assumptions that are celebrated in a globalized world. Systems thinkers refer to these qualities as structural reasons for the continuation of growth.

Questions to Consider

1. Does your nation want to continually grow the economy? What are the dangers of this way of thinking? What are the benefits?
2. Why do people worry that it will be a disaster if the economy doesn't grow?

4. Information

In a global economy, information is added to the economic mix of land, labor, and capital. **Information** is specific data or particular services applied to a product, service, or activity that adds monetary value. Some examples of value-added information are services from advertisers, lawyers, marketers, accountants, insurance, financiers, efficiency experts, risk analysts, and computer applications. The purpose of adding information is to maximize productivity, profitability and efficiency, and attract recognition to a product or service in an intensely competitive world.[11] Information in the globalized economy is not just applied for societal well-being, but also to maximize profit.

A **sharing economy** takes a variety of forms, often leveraging information technology to enable individuals, corporations, non-profits and government with information to efficiently distribute, share, and reuse the excess capacity in goods and services. This sharing economy succeeds because of a depressed labor market, in which many people supplement their income by commodifying

their property and labor in different ways. People join the sharing economy because they may have lost a full-time job, including a few cases where the pricing structure of the sharing economy may have made their old jobs less profitable. For example, full-time taxi drivers may switch to be Uber drivers. The Uber transportation company develops, markets and operates the Uber mobile app, which allows consumers to submit a trip request that is linked to the network of Uber drivers. Uber is displacing traditional economy taxi drivers and companies with mostly part-time, independent contractor workers who use their own car to transport people for extra income. The real economic benefit goes to the privately owned Uber Corporation and its shareholders, currently worth $50 billion, which takes in a big slice of the profits.[12]

5. Labor and Economic Globalization

The 1941 Stolper-Samuelson theorem explains labor trends accompanying the spread of economic globalization, as well as trade. It basically says that the effect of trade between a core (rich) nation and a periphery (poor) nation is that the wages for the unskilled labor force in the core nation will be lower because they are competing globally with unskilled workers in a periphery nation. This theorem is currently being played out in the U.S. and other core countries. Since the 1980s, 2 ½ billion people in China, India, Eastern Europe, and the former Soviet Union have discarded economic isolationism and joined the global economy. When the global economy added these workers, wages fell across the board. When a core, capital-abundant country (such as the U.S.) trades with a labor-abundant country (such as China), wages in the core country fall and corporate profits go up.

Cartoon from Pinterest

The theorem's economic logic is simple. Free trade is tantamount to a massive increase in the core country's labor supply, since the products made by periphery country workers can now be imported. Additionally, demand for workers in the core country falls as corporations shift labor-intensive production to a periphery country. The net result is an increase in the labor supply and a decrease in labor demand in the core country; thus wages fall.[13] Economist Thomas Palley notes, "Now, this shift is coming together in the form of a 'super-sized' Stolper-Samuelson effect, and has depressing consequences for American workers."[14] Adding 2 ½ billion people from low-wage countries to the global labor market is an unprecedented event.

Samuelson questioned the benefits of economic globalization for labor. With the emergence of China, India, and Eastern Europe, the dam of isolation holding back 2 ½ billion workers from the global economic workforce has been removed. If two swimming pools are joined, the water level will eventually equalize. A threat to labor is competition. Manufacturing workers in core countries are already competing with technological innovations as well as labor from periphery countries, with dire consequences for manufacturing workers in the core countries. Samuelson claimed "that since U.S. labor has lost its old monopoly on American advanced know-how and capital, free trade could indeed lower the share of wages in the U.S. GDP and increase overall inequality."[15]

Outsourcing involves the contracting out of a business function to an external provider, usually to a low-wage country. One of the reasons for the rapid decline in manufacturing jobs in core countries is the outsourcing of jobs to low-wage periphery countries, such as China, Mexico, Indonesia, India, and Vietnam. The same is happening to professional and higher-paid workers in core countries with similar effects. Outsourcing is not just the province of the manufacturing sector, but includes professionals in software, banking, insurance, pharmaceuticals, and engineering. Therefore, in core countries most of the new jobs are in highly skilled occupations or domestic services and low-paying retail work.[16] The middle has been hollowed out.

6. Technology

Technological changes have ushered in faster and more sophisticated communication and transportation technologies that transcend national boundaries and more intricately connect the world than at any time in the past. These instantaneous high-speed communication devices with sophisticated computer technologies revolutionize our relations with each other. The Internet, television, high-speed travel, cell phones, and other forms of telecommunications link the world by dissolving former barriers of time and distance and provide new connections between people. But on a downside, the extreme gap between the global rich and poor is due in large part to technology and economic globalization.

A GLOBALIZED SOCIETY

Since the economy is global in scope, the class structure is as well. A global economy has changed the class structure that was formerly nation-based to one that is now globally based. The American economy has been in the midst of a sea change, shifting from industry to services and information technology and integrating itself far more tightly into a single, global market for goods, labor, and capital. China, India, and other middle countries have emerged as economic competitors, capable of producing large volumes of high-value, low-priced goods and services. This transformation has been underway since the 1980s, but the pace of change has quickened since 2000 and even more so since the 2008 financial crisis.[17]

For core nations, the hollowing out of the middle class way of life has taken place since the 1980s, with the double-edged onslaught of four developments that favor the wealthy: technological innovations, neoliberalism, financialization and economic globalization. Along with the hollowing out of the American middle class, there has taken place a surge in the formation of a middle class in

Brazil, Russia, India, China, and South Africa (BRICS), and other countries.

The wealthy have designed the rules of neoliberalism and economic globalization to benefit them; they encourage competition among countries for business, which drives down taxes on corporations, weakens health and environmental protections, and undermines labor rights, such as collective bargaining.[18] On the other hand, policies that favor the middle class—higher income tax rates on the wealthy, ample funding for education, low-interest loans for education, research and development that encourage job creation, a fair inheritance tax rate, tax deductions for home ownership, a safety net for economic hardships, and pensions for retirement—have all been eroding since 1980.[19] Also, the formation and thriving of small businesses have been hampered by "big box" retailers such as Walmart that undercut their smaller rivals.

Middle class in China, photo Denise Ames

The global middle class consists of one billion individuals. They have average wealth per adult of $10,000 to $100,000 and own one-sixth of global wealth. Almost 60 percent or 587 million individuals in the middle segment are located in Asia Pacific, the fastest-growing economies. The middle class of this region is expected to replace the indebted U.S. middle class households as the global growth locomotive.[20] The middle class expanded in Asia Pacific countries and shrunk in many core and other periphery countries mostly because countries simply stopped making things and started buying them from the Asian Pacific countries. Since 2000, the U.S. has lost over 3 million manufacturing jobs; Brazil has lost 2 million since 1998, and South Africa has lost nearly 1 million. In the past, Argentina assembled televisions; now it purchases most of them from abroad. Mozambique in Africa packaged its cashew crop 30 years ago; today the country ships its raw nuts overseas for others to bottle and can. Zambians made their own clothes in the 1980s; now they sort through bundles of clothes shipped from the U.S. and Europe. The Hunters Point neighborhood in San Francisco, California (US) manufactured the ships that delivered American-made goods to the world; now the ships docked in the Bay Area's ports are mostly from East Asia, unloading foreign-made products for U.S. consumers.[21]

Increasingly, in some countries the workplace is more central to social life than the family. Family members are spending more time at work or school or going to and from work than in the home. Many critics contend that the workplace has evolved into a substitute family. Generally, both men and women spend more time at work than with their families, resulting in personal workplace relationships. While the workplace offers rewards, acceptance, and recognition that are often missing in family relationships, it can also be shattering to an individual if his/her workplace ceases operation or if s/he is terminated from a job. Some critics argue that work consumes so much family energy and time that in many cases family life is an empty shell. Instead of creating their own viable family life with all the accompanying trials and tribulations, many individuals turn to television, computers, and social media as a fantasy replacement for family life. As a substitute family, the workplace fails to provide the stability, continuity, and acceptance that a healthy family traditionally furnishes.

With growing temporary employment stints, job uncertainty, and telecommuting, the workplace is not a source of stability and security needed by individuals; thus, many people feel more insecure, uncertain, anxious, alienated, and fragmented.

POLITICAL GLOBALIZATION

Politically, nations are no longer the only defining political entity. The nation state still exists as a workable political organization but can no longer deal in isolation with complex problems—terrorism, environmental pollution, weapons proliferation, conflict resolution, disease control, drug proliferation, and migration—that disregard local, regional, and national boundaries and can only be addressed on a trans-national basis. Nations share their former exclusive sovereignty, in varying degrees, with other world organizations. These organizations include the United Nations (UN), World Court, the World Trade Organization (WTO), and World Bank; regional organizations such as the North Atlantic Treaty Organization (NATO) and European Union (EU); and regional trade alliances like the North American Free Trade Association (NAFTA). Human rights agencies such as Amnesty International, humanitarian agencies such as Red Cross and Doctors without Borders, and environmental watchdog groups like Greenpeace and Sierra Club also meet global challenges. Sometimes nations, such as the United States, balk at giving up their sovereignty to join with others in fostering mutual world cooperation.

Multi-national corporations play a significant political role in the globalized world as well. They, in many cases, seduce local, state, and national politicians with campaign donations or outright bribes to formulate policies and laws that favor their profitable undertakings.

Terrorists attack the World Trade Center, New York, USA

Democracy struggles to become the favored political structure and liberalism the preferred political philosophy in much of the world. Yet, many attempts to establish democracy in nations such as Egypt, Syria, Libya, and China have failed. Nations struggling to unify, stabilize, and participate in the world economy are encouraged by the West to adopt democracy as a form of political organization. Many social justice groups fight the oligarchic tendencies of global corporations to ensure that their nations do indeed retain democratic institutions, and that the form of democracy embraced by emerging nations is not just a facade for the real corporate powers that operate behind the scenes.

From a globalized worldview, conflict and warfare are different from the modern worldview. Conflict has become unpredictable, random, irrational, and volatile. Wars can be sparked by many factors, among them: scarce resources like water, food, fuel, or other basic necessities; religious differences and perspectives; different worldviews; exploitation by core nations; and tensions and anxieties created by rapid social disruption with the accompanying loss of solidifying traditions and customs. Recent terrorists' attacks by marginalized people resisting modernization and globalization are examples of conflict in a globalized world.

CULTURAL GLOBALIZATION

Consumerism is touted as a new "world religion." Led by the U.S., a vast entertainment and advertising sector has perpetuated and glamorized the notion of consumerism as a form of status and as a symbol of affiliation with modern culture. Rampant consumerism has gone way beyond the basic products for a comfortable material life to the frenzied accumulation of consumer items that purportedly bring an individual psychological well-being and status recognition.

The globalized worldview is reflected in mainstream American thought in what I label the "consumer creed." The principles of the consumer creed are generally accepted by a vast majority of Americans who have energetically exported it to others throughout the world, such as India and China. It includes: the desire for a comfortable life-style with a profusion of consumer comforts; an attitude of economic progress in which hard work is blessed with ample financial rewards; a

right to material abundance without concern for the environmental costs or for the welfare of those who provide these goods and services; a competitive, ambitious, individualistic value system; a professional or entrepreneurial career preference where wealth is realized without regard for how it is obtained; faith in technological progress as the means to solve all problems; a disconnect between our materialistic/consumer way of life and its effects upon the environment; and the attitude that this "consumer creed" is the highest ideal and this way of life should be shared with the rest of the world. Without regard for future generations, the consumer creed has left many people discontented, alienated, unfulfilled, and in a spiritual malaise while leaving the planet environmentally ravaged.

A common language acts as a unifying factor, and English is increasingly that universal language. The world's elites speak English in part because of the influence of the British in the 19th century and the hegemony of the U.S. in the 20th century. English, the language of business, commerce, and education, is the unofficial language of those holding a globalized worldview.

Accompanying the sophistication and expansion of computer technology is the availability of an overwhelming amount of information. Technological and economic developments have outpaced our cultural and social responses, often leaving us confused about how to make sense of this overwhelming influx of information and rapid change. Intense debates rage among diverse religious, civic, environmental, and other concerned groups about the future; some are problematic as the dialogue descends into acts of incivility. Others see the debates as a reaction to complex changes and anxiety brought about by rapid technological and economic developments and future uncertainty.

One key change in communication is the deemphasizing of face-to-face, interpersonal communication. Technological devices—smart cell phones, texting, email, Twitter, Facebook, and on-line courses—erase the boundaries of time and space that had previously slowed and restricted communication by fostering instant communication with anyone in the world. These forms of communication connect people removed from their social and physical environment, but also separate interactions from the social spaces in which people physically exist. In this way, technological forms of communication contribute to the annihilation of the public space which had connected people with one another. For example, a huge trend in education is on-line or distance learning courses, in which students do not attend a traditional classroom but complete the subject material on the computer through an on-line program. The direct, inter-personal exchange between students and instructor is eliminated and displaced by on-line communication.[22] Our attention is no longer directed only to those within the confines of our physical space but beyond it. We can become isolated islands in the public sphere, separated from others by our technological wonders.

Many cultural expressions—music, dance, art, entertainment, literature, film, and dress—have been made into commodities for the world consumer market and follow a distinctive Western commercial bent. Mass produced shows featuring a renowned celebrity can command premium prices for star-packed spectacles. Entertainment can range from celebrity singers to Broadway musicals and plays, comedians, musicians, and stage acts. All have in common a hefty price that globalized viewers are willing to pay. Dazzling sets and astonishing effects provide manufactured excitement. In the art world, sophisticated buyers with fistfuls of cash are intent upon purchasing

authentic and unique art pieces that distinguish them as connoisseurs of fine art. Many are collectors of one of a kind memorabilia ranging from old movie posters to out-of-print books, rare coins, Superman comics, or antique furniture. Undoubtedly the collections bring pleasure to the collectors, but collecting still involves commodification of items and attaching monetary value to them. Critics of the commercialized entertainment industry maintain that there is no interaction between the performer and the audience. Instead the audience merely observes the performance and responds through admiring applause. The entertainer then packs up the show to present the exact same performance in another locale in a franchise-like duplication of artistic services. The result is a "McDonaldization" of the entertainment industry.

CONCLUDING INSIGHTS: THE GLOBALIZED WORLDVIEW

The best-established, mainstream ideology in the U.S. and many parts of the world (including China) is the globalized worldview. The universalization and homogenization of a commodified and commercialized globalized culture has expanded since the 1980s. This globalized culture is increasingly being accepted and replicated by many people, with businesses encouraging consumerism as an embodiment of universal culture. For example, over 500,000 foreign students attend American universities. This education and socialization process enfolds foreign students into a globalized culture, which many enthusiastically embrace and take back with them to their country of origin. Millions of middle class Chinese and Indians enthusiastically purchase cars and other material goods that traditionally were associated with the West. Also, the ubiquitous satellite dishes perched on roofs around the world beam commercially laden television programs direct from

Hollywood and Seoul, South Korea to the homes of billions around the world. Television programs implicitly extol the values of a globalized worldview in their programming selections and blatant commercialism.

As we have seen in this chapter, the globalization worldview has both negative and beneficial aspects. One of the most disturbing aspects of a globalized worldview in my view is a gradual loss of cultural diversity that results in monotone cultural conformity around the world revolving around a consumerist and technological mindset. Many people are immersed in their own virtual world with little outward connection to others or nature. On the other hand, technology has enabled us to connect with others across time and space in a way that can foster greater communication in solving intractable global problems.

How do we balance the beneficial aspects of a globalized worldview with the negative? This fundamental question is what those embracing a transformative worldview will have to sort out. Let's turn to the transformative worldview chapter to find out what some people have in store for a more sustainable future.

CHAPTER SIX

The Transformative Worldview

"For the first time in human evolution, the individual life is long enough, and the cultural transformation swift enough, that the individual mind is now a constituent player in the global transformation of human culture."

— William Irwin Thompson

AN INTRODUCTION TO THE TRANSFORMATIVE WORLDVIEW

At this point in time, millions of diverse people around the world are actively calling for a different worldview. Some say a different story is urgently needed to assure the continuation of our human species and life as we know it on Earth. Some people in diverse fields—educators, religious leaders, business entrepreneurs, international political leaders, indigenous farmers, political activists, politicians, environmentalists, entertainers, scientists, working people, artists, writers, small business owners, academics, economists, concerned citizens, and many others—are contributing to the creation of what I call a transformative worldview. Those who adhere to a transformative worldview, at least in part, imagine that diverse paths are possible and attainable, and a globalized worldview or other visions of the future are not an inevitable scenario of how the future will or should be played out. They are promoting alternative ideas and diverse options for a different worldview and voicing their convictions in a forceful, yet usually peaceful fashion.

Wise elders, !Kung woman, Africa, photo Izla Bardavid

Elements in the formation of a transformative worldview come from diverse sources; some are positive aspects of the four other worldviews. For example, highly regarded from the indigenous worldview is the wisdom of indigenous people who call upon the wise council of their elders, respect and connect with nature, draw on the support of extended family, and value the strong relationship with territorial place. From the modern worldview is gleaned the ideal of liberal democracy, the advancement of scientific inquiry, medical improvements, beneficial technological innovations, public-supported mass education, and progress in the expansion of human rights to include women and people of color; all are noteworthy accomplishments. From the fundamentalist worldview comes the close connection to family and community and the recognition of a greater power than individualism alone. The stunning technological developments from the globalized worldview, especially high-speed, integrated computer networks, and reasonably-priced global transportation have provided instantaneous communication linking diverse people around the globe. Even some indigenous people in remote villages are linked to the internet and use appropriate scientific knowledge for enhancing their own goal of self-

Computer technology in Rwanda, Africa

sufficiency in food consumption. And some would say that the globalized worldview's vision of "opening up" the world to unfettered trade has benefited many people with a more materially comfortable standard of living than ever experienced before.

All of these worldviews have some positive contributions in creating a different worldview, but those advancing a transformative worldview believe that there needs to be selectivity and mindfulness in fitting values of the four other worldviews into a new framework. Therefore, a different worldview needs to continue its evolution and offer alternatives to prevailing notions of cultural

The Transformative Worldview: 10 Characteristics

1. **Interdependent Ideals** are emerging that focus on interdependence, cooperation, community, connections, support, and altruism rather than greed, aggression, independence, and segmentation. Other descriptors of the transformative worldview include simultaneity, uncertainty, relationship, networks, webs, integration, and diversity.

2. **Community-Focused Social Values** draw upon the wisdom of our elders and their experiential insights. Intense individualism is a learned, aggressive behavior, historically created and promoted by Western society, especially the U.S. A shift to a worldview emphasizing greater cooperative, supportive, and life-enhancing attributes is a viable alternative.

Sustainable agriculture, Mexico, photo Denise Ames

3. **Natural Capitalism** places priority on the well-being and sustainability of the Earth. It includes socially responsible investing, social entrepreneurship, micro-credit banking, community development, local businesses, self-managed worker-run enterprises, cooperatives, non-profit organizations, and other forms of management in which individuals have a vested interest in profitability and outcomes.

4. **Ecological Awareness** has awakened our insight into the interdependence of everything in nature, where every event has an effect on everything else. Humans are part of the mystery of the Universe and not isolated, separate, and superior entities.

5. **Renewable Energy** in the form of wind, solar, water, steam, and others is important in countering the dire effects of climate change and stimulating economic development. The devastation caused by a fossil fuel-dependent lifestyle has galvanized world citizens to start shifting from oil and coal dependence to sustainable energy.

6. **Peace and Justice Movements** connect millions of people instantly with world-wide communication networks. These vigorous movements include democratic reforms, peace efforts, nuclear disarmament, population control, human rights, animal rights, LGBT rights, environmental issues, educational reforms, equality, rights for indigenous people, women's and children's issues, and others.

7. **Sustainable Agriculture** is a shift from industrial agricultural that is no longer able to meet the world's food needs to local and organic farming.

8. **Holistic Health** offers alternatives to Western medicine that is often dominated by a for-profit pharmaceutical industry and invasive medical procedures. It encourages health, well-being, a mostly plant-based diet and a holistic way to cure diseases ranging from cancer to heart disease.

9. **Spirituality** includes alternative practices that differ from traditional religious practices. Many traditional religions have accommodated the desire expressed by many people for more connected and personal spiritual experiences rather than rote adherence to prescribed creeds and rituals.

10. **Holistic Education** is the key to ushering in alternative changes. Holistic educational practices for adults and youth encourage multi-culturalism, open-mindedness and diversity, inquiry-based learning, multiple intelligences, a global perspective, and a holistic world history!

uniformity, rigid fundamentalism, corporate dominance, consumer-driven values, selfish individualism, oligarchic concentration of wealth and power, political stalemate, and environmental destruction. Even though those who embrace a transformative worldview have a diverse array of thoughts, beliefs, ideas, theories, lifestyles, choices, and actions that defy rigid categorization, they do share common principles and ideals that I have placed under the umbrella of a transformative worldview.

The transformative worldview is still a minority view, but it is a worldwide movement in which millions of people are reassessing the values of the other worldviews in order to find a more compassionate, equal, sustainable, and community-focused value system. I have organized 10 characteristics (see above) that briefly describe the emerging transformative worldview in the U.S. and across the world.

The transformative worldview is further explained through six patterns—cultural, political, social, economic, technological, and ecological—outlined below.

CULTURAL PATTERNS

Many people hold to new and emerging transformative ideals such as cooperation, community, and holistic thinking. **Holistic** means that all the traits of a culture—economic, technological, social, political, religious, ideological, and cultural—interact and reinforce each other. It also sees the world as an intricately interconnected organism; accentuates uncertainty, approximations, and relativity instead of absolutes; calls for interdependence instead of independence; and recognizes seemingly paradoxical concepts. Highly regarded are Eastern philosophies and religious thought that emphasize cyclical thinking, highlight harmony with nature, and see unity within diversity and diversity within unity.[1] A holistic perspective recognizes that nature, which has

Gaia, our Earth

been treated for centuries as dead and mechanical, is an animate, invisible organizing power. The Earth, Gaia, is seen as a living organism interconnected within a web of life. This perspective counters the split between nature and humans which threatens life on Earth. A holistic view intuits that an underlying consciousness circulates within humans, life on Earth, and the Universe connecting all into an intricate, interdependent circle of existence.

Many holding a transformative worldview are embracing alternative forms of spirituality that depart from the universal religions that arose over 5,000 years ago. A **New Age movement**, emerging out of the West in the 1960s and 1970s, is an umbrella term that embraces an eclectic array of spiritual beliefs and practices. It encompasses a wide range of personal development strategies and healing tactics to improve human well-being. Deepak Chopra, spiritual teacher, states that New Age values support conscious evolution, a non-sectarian society, a non-military culture, global sharing, healing the environment, sustainable economies, self-determination, social justice, economic empowerment of the poor, love, and compassion in action.

Many women have resurrected feminist spirituality that encourages a connection with the sacred feminine and worship of the goddess that they claim has been suppressed by male-dominated universal religions. My cousin, a practicing shaman, performs rituals for clients and friends, such as fire ceremonies, that she contends burns away negative feelings and evil entities resulting in a cleansing of the soul and renewal of positive energy.

The field of **ecopsychology**, connecting psychology with ecology, offers many people a way to spiritually connect with Mother Earth. Ecopsychologists maintain that this emotional connection between individuals and the natural world will help them develop sustainable and simple life-styles and remedy alienation from nature. They support preserving nature on public lands, bringing nature into civic spaces, and connecting nature to their own personal space. Instead of the traditional lawn of green grass and shrubs, my neighbor has a menagerie of native plants that provides a welcome sanctuary for birds and other wildlife.

In some ways, post-modernism is part of the transformative worldview. Although I described post-modernism more fully in the modern world-view chapter, its rejection of the modern worldview also can place it within the transformative camp. Post-modern thinkers of the 20th century deconstructed the objective, scientific, modern worldview that has held sway for centuries and instead posited that there is no fixed meaning, canon, tradition, or objectivity; only infinity of meaning. This way of thinking erodes classical, rational liberalism, the cornerstone of the modern worldview.[2]

Aesthetic expression in a transformative worldview differs from the globalized worldview. In many instances, the distance between the observer/observed or entertainer/entertained is reduced or eliminated. A person does not go to a concert and sit passively as the observer but may participate in the musical production by performing themselves or helping with the production. For example, a dancer in the audience might spontaneously participate in the dancing. The professional qualities that make certain artists celebrities are blurred and the boundaries between the performer and audience fall away. A small, neighborhood performance-theater in Pennsylvania, for example, featured audience participation as they followed sing-a-long tunes reminiscent of the 1960s "Sing-a-Long with Mitch" television show. The audience was the performer. Another example is the self-publishing book industry, which has recently skyrocketed. The big publishing houses no longer dictate what will be available to the book-buying public. Instead, individual authors can "self- publish" their own books, freed of restrictions imposed by corporate publishing entities. Also, blogs, tweets, and other forms of social media are not governed by established rules, but authors can publish whatever they determine is important to them.

POLITICAL PATTERNS

The transformative worldview advocates for a decrease in the dominance of the nation-state arrangement. Other political configurations are emerging to challenge or complement the sovereignty of the nation state. The organization, structure, and services that governments provide for their citizenry are changing markedly because of the shift by many nations from managed capitalism and socialism to neoliberalism and state capitalism. With more wealth concentrated in the hands of the elite, politicians have increasingly supported policies that favor the wealthy. Although the political organization in the U.S. is a republic with democratically elected representatives, increasingly we see that democracy is divided into two contending segments that I call elite democracy and participatory democracy.

Many in the transformative movement favor involvement in participatory democracy for the

Clean elections

benefit of all, not elite democracy where a few wealthy oligarchs dominant the political agenda. For example, a movement for what are called Clean Elections strives to make elections publicly funded from government sources and small constituent donations instead of from wealthy corporations and individuals who expect favorable responses to their agenda from "their" elected politicians. My hometown of Albuquerque, New Mexico, for example, passed Clean Election regulations for local elections in 2005.

Peace and justice movements have had renewed vigor since the invention of the internet and world-wide communication. There are many local peace and justice chapters that encourage local engagement. For example, I am a member of the Albuquerque Center for Peace and Justice. With their ability to connect millions of people instantly, the issues of peace, and social and economic justice are garnering attention and action. Among some

of the many causes advocated by this diverse movement include democratic reforms, peace efforts, nuclear disarmament, population control, human rights, animal rights, gay rights, equality for non-elites, indigenous people's rights, women's and children's issues, racial

equality, and protection from hate crimes. These causes are moral and ethical standards that guide nation's policies and action. For example, advocacy groups in the United States are lobbying for a Department of Peace to balance the Department of Defense's enormous financial outlays and influ-

United Nations, New York City

ence.

World institutions and organizations are gaining more authority and legitimacy as they try to complement the authority of the nation-state. During the 20th century, world political institutions evolved that reflected a more interdependent world. One of the first such institutions, the League of Nations established after World War I in 1920, failed to prevent the outbreak of World War II, although its successor, the United Nations (UN), has proven to be a more successful organization and has a peacekeeping wing to enforce its objectives. International political entities today include world, regional, non-governmental organizations (NGOs), and citizen-diplomat groups. International organizations, such as the already mentioned UN and the International Court, are charged with the overwhelming task of helping to stamp out terrorism, regulate

arms, monitor human rights, prevent disease and hunger, and protect the environment. The WTO, World Bank, and IMF are global institutions charged with governing the global economy.

Non-governmental organizations (NGOs) are privately created organizations with an international scope, unaffiliated with a particular nation. According to political scientist Farouk Mawlawi, NGOs are "private, voluntary, non-profit organizations whose members combine their skills, means and energies in the service of shared ideals and objectives."[3] NGOs transcend narrow national inter-ests in dealing with issues affecting the world and include such well-known world organizations as the Red Cross, Amnesty International, Greenpeace, Doctors' Without Borders, and Human Rights Watch. Many of these organi-zations have local and state chapters for easy engagement by ordinary citizens.

Regional political organizations complement nation-al governments. A regional organization like the North Atlantic Treaty Organization (NATO) has taken on new objectives along with its primary Cold War goal of pro-tecting Western Europe. The Organization of American States (OAS), established in 1948 with 21 members, is the oldest regional organization of states. The European

Human Rights Watch, an NGO

Union (EU), a regional organization of currently 27 member nations, has achieved a cooperative economy, has its own currency, the euro, and has removed tariff barriers for easier trade. Formed in 2001, the African Union has 54 members on the African continent. One of its objectives is the pro-motion and protection of human rights, such as the right of a group to freely dispose of its natural resources in the exclusive interest of its members. In 1945, Egypt, Jordan, Iraq, Lebanon, Syria and Saudi Arabia signed the Pact of the Arab League States and created the League of Arab States with 22 members in 2011. The League of Arab States is separate from the Organization of the Islamic Conference, which was the second largest inter-governmental organization in 2011, with 57 mem-ber states, just below the UN in membership. The Association of Southeast Asian Nations (ASEAN) has 10 members and was formed in 1967.

SOCIAL PATTERNS

Some people adhering to a transformative worldview see the rights of indigenous people, women, non-elites, animals, and the environment as worthy of promoting. Some people earnestly work to-wards eradicating racism, sexism, classism, and homophobia around the world. Since around the 1990s, for example, **LBGT movements**, a term that did not exist before 1990, have been achieving human rights for lesbian, bisexual, gay, transgender and transsexual people around the world. The LGBT social movement advocates for the equalized accep-tance of LGBT people in society. Although there is not an overarching central organization that rep-resents all LGBT people and their interests, many organizations are active worldwide. Today these movements include political activism and cultural activity, including lobbying, street marches, social

LGBT rainbow

groups, media, art, and research. The 1990s saw a rapid push of the transgender movement, and it continues today.

Many people who promote a transformative worldview believe that education is the key to ushering in alternative changes. Some wish to deinstitutionalize our educational establishments and make our schools diverse, engaging, and beneficial to all, not just an elite group. They are critical of No Child Left Behind that overemphasizes testing and "punishes" schools that "fail" to meet arbitrary national standards. Popular among many educators (including this author) are holistic educational practices that encourage diversity, inquiry-based learning, activities that connect with our multiple intelligences, a global perspective, and a holistic world history!

The importance of communal values, rather than an over emphasis on individualism as the central cultural value is important to many people connecting with the transformative worldview. Emerging social values can be gathered from contemporary culture, from diverse ancient traditions, and from our own imaginations. For example, we can learn to draw upon the wisdom of our elders and their historical insights. Intense individualism is a learned behavior historically created and promoted by Western society, especially the United States. Those who support a transformative worldview believe a shift to a worldview that emphasizes greater cooperative, supportive, and life-enhancing attributes is a viable and necessary alternative. Visionary Mary Clark notes, "We urgently need to reinstate feelings of relatedness and community into our social vision."[4]

Extended family, Spain

The negative and positive effects of rapid social changes in the 20th century and early 21st century are playing out today. Our society is fraying at the edges because of social fragmentation and alienation. The social structures that are in place in the U.S. today widen the income gap, perpetuate poverty, alienate individuals and families, foster rampant individualism, and encourage the growth of a consumer society at great cost to the environment and individual well-being. When these seemingly intractable problems are looked at from a holistic perspective, they can be addressed more effectively. We are constantly blaming groups or individuals for "causing" these problems: politicians blame teachers for not educating students satisfactorily, teachers blame parents for not providing a good foundation for education, liberals blame television and social media for "dumbing-down" students, and advertisers say just be "cool" and all is well. Yet the whole system is out of balance.

The values and beliefs of the modern and globalized worldview govern our social system. Some supporters of the transformative worldview say our society drives us to pursue individual rewards, pleasures, and recognition, while the family, community, and commons are devalued and rendered subservient to the individual. Children are trucked to day-care centers so that parents can earn money in the marketplace that takes them away from the home and their children. Even when there is enough leisure time for family or community enjoyment, it frequently revolves around the marketplace providing platforms for entertainment. The adage "it takes a village to raise a child" has been replaced by "it takes a day care to raise a child."

The indigenous worldview provides valuable insights into societal readjustments. Historically, the band, group, family, village, clan, and tribe have provided mechanisms for human belonging.

Humans have a universal, innate sense of wanting to belong to something bigger than just themselves. It is in our deep collective unconscious to live in connection with each other; it has only been recently that we have deviated from this norm. Instead, there has been a shift from the community to the individual. This has intensified since the end of World War II and further intensified since the 1980s, when the ideal of the individual has reigned supreme. Now rampant individualism has reached a crisis point. Social disengagement and alienation are expressed in the upsurge in the use of anti-depressant drugs, the rash of teen suicides, and an untold number of broken families. For example, from 2001 to 2014 there was a 2.8-fold increase in the total number of prescription drug deaths. We have become untethered to our innate human need—the need to belong.

For individual well-being, those supporting a transformative worldview argue that our social patterns need to change to a more equitable, nourishing, and sustainable way of life. The good news is that many people recognize this is an urgent issue and are remaking social institutions to foster more community spirit and rethinking the self-serving individualism that permeates the values and attitudes of many parts of American and world society. For example, many religious institutions are once again encouraging their places of worship to provide a setting for social interaction and support for their members and others in the community. Changing parts of the system can trigger changes in the whole system. It is a huge challenge, but once awareness is reached, change can come about. Perhaps once again we will be able to claim that it takes a village to raise a child.

Questions to Consider

1. What does the saying "it takes a village to raise a child" mean to you?

ECONOMIC PATTERNS

Those holding a transformative worldview believe in creating a more just, equitable and sustainable economy that places less stress on an overtaxed environment. They are trying to counter the damage from global capitalism and its related values of greed and consumption that have been inflicted upon the human psyche. Many individuals and organizations struggle to eliminate free trade agreements such as NAFTA (North American Free Trade Agreement) and the WTO (World Trade Organization) that have wreaked havoc on local economies, workers, small businesses, and the environment, while enriching multinational corporations and their shareholders. Instead, many people are working to reinstate bilateral trade agreements, where each trading nation makes its own mutually beneficial trade agreements. Other people are working to set-up alternative business forms such as non-profit businesses, cooperatives, and local, community, or employee-owned enterprises.

Local business, Buckhannon, West Virginia, USA

For example, a committed group of individuals in my local community are working to establish a community-owned bank in which the state and local governments deposits their excess funds. The profits from this enterprise are channeled back into the local community rather than to out-of-state investors. Many people struggle to break the corporate lock on the "economic imagination" and develop diverse enterprises in which workers have a stake in their workplace and the sustainability of the Earth is given utmost consideration.

Some people argue that we can more effectively deal with the extraordinary rate of economic change by actively participating in life choices and not permitting the "consumer creed" that was explained in the globalized worldview to dictate our options. Natural capitalism, which places priority on the well-being and sustainability of the Earth, is among the many economic changes emerging. Other significant economic changes include socially responsible investing, social entrepreneurship, micro-credit banking, community development, local businesses, self-managed worker-run enterprises, cooperative enterprises, non-profit organizations, disinvestment measures, and others. For example, some people on college campuses are calling on college financial administrators to disinvest their investments from the fossil fuel industry. There is also a renewed call for stricter financial sector regulations, a cap on excessive executive compensation, breaking up large corporate holdings, and other reforms.

One alternative to the globalized economy is the redevelopment of the once flourishing local or domestic economy. Local community members, government officials, and business owners can alleviate the wealth depletion of the local economy by returning to "economic self-determination." This return to local capitalism reduces dependency on multinational corporations, while creating wealth-accumulating enterprises at the local level. Local economies can produce, market, and process many of their own products for local or regional consumption, reducing transportation and middleman costs. **Local capitalism** can bring local economies into harmony with the surrounding ecosystem, foster cooperation within the community, and substitute more personalized local products for more expensive imported and often sub-standard goods. In order for such a change to occur, the real effort must come from the local community that can better utilize available resources in imaginative ways and provide more economical and high quality food, clothing, shelter, transportation, and energy. A transfer of economic interests and activities from urban, core centers to the local community can reduce dependency on the core and revive local economic vibrancy.[5]

Organic greenhouse farming

Concerns are arising over the fact that our industrial form of agricultural production is no longer able to meet the needs of the world's population. Along with industrial agriculture's enormous demands for irrigation water, its chemical inputs deplete the fertility of the soil and its fossil fuel dependency contributes to climate change. Alternatives to mass-produced, industrial agriculture are emerging, such as the rise of sustainable, organic, and local agriculture. An alternative to industrial agriculture, organic farming connects what one eats to how one lives. It also considers the person charged with spraying destructive chemicals on foods and the considerable harm done to his/her health.

A number of communities scattered throughout the world are working to incrementally achieve the goal of more local businesses rooted in the community. For example, in the United States, a worker-owned initiative is located in the economically hard-hit city of Cleveland, Ohio.

The "Cleveland Model" involves an integrated array of worker-owned cooperative enterprises targeted at the $3 billion purchasing power of such large scale "anchor institutions" as the Cleveland Clinic, University Hospital, and Case Western Reserve University. The association of enterprises also includes a revolving fund so that profits made by the businesses help establish new ventures. A worker-owned company, Evergreen Cooperative Laundry, is a state-of-the-art commercial laundry that provides clean linens for area hospitals, nursing homes, and hotels. It includes 50 worker-

owners, pays above-market wages, provides health insurance, and is still able to compete successfully against other commercial laundries. Another enterprise, Ohio Cooperative Solar (OCS), provides weatherization services and installs, owns, and maintains solar panels. Each year, two to four new worker-owned ventures are planned for opening. A 20-acre land trust will own the land of the worker-owned businesses.[6] A revitalization of the local economy does not mean isolation and a complete rejection of the global capitalist economy but incorporating both the global and the local economy.

Green city growers

TECHNOLOGICAL PATTERNS

Some people supporting a transformative worldview dispute the notion that scientific progress and our faith in technological fixes can solve all complex problems and make the world a better, safer place to live. Instead, it is a tacit understanding that science, technology, and a consumer-materialistic way of life have certain limitations and repercussions for our human species as well as for other life forms on Earth. However, most people in the transformative movement realize the importance

of internet and computer technology in instantaneously linking and organizing people around the world, while also providing accurate and transparent information.

Even though technology cannot fix all problems, perhaps it can help us deal with some of the urgent issues. But, instead of using technology as the latest consumer fad, we need the wisdom to direct the technology to positive ends. As we have found in world history, one thing that humans are good at is making tools. Sometimes the repercussions of our tool-making creations are not immediately apparent; the atomic and nuclear bombs come to mind as inventions that have few, if any, re-

Wind turbines

deeming qualities. But many inventions have been beneficial—the Internet has certainly benefited me. Many new innovations are underway to help "clean-up" the environment, bring more energy efficiency to our way of life, and treat medical issues. Perhaps technology will provide the tools we need to save ourselves—but not without the vision to tell us how to use them.

ENVIRONMENTAL PATTERNS

Those holding a transformative worldview treat the environment not just as an economic commodity but feel that the Earth must be healthy to sustain humans and our fellow species. This view represents a shift in attitude that has been gaining momentum throughout the world. A new ecological awareness has awakened the perception of the interdependence of everything in nature, where every event has an effect on everything else. Humans are seen as part of the mystery of the Universe and not isolated, separate, superior entities. With this awareness comes responsibility along with an urgency to repair the damage done to the environment and halt further environmental destruction. For example, even tourism has taken an ecological turn for many travelers who opt for popular ecotourism destinations such as Costa Rica and Belize. Ecotourism means visiting fragile, pristine, and relatively undeveloped natural areas, it is intended as a low-impact and small scale alternative to large scale, commercial tourism.

The human population has grown exponentially in the 20th century and continues to be an urgent issue in the 21st century. The carrying capacity of the Earth is severely strained by our current population. Will our Earth be able to sustain 9 to 12 billion people, a number projected to occur around 2050? If the 9 to 12 billion people projected to live on this earth in 2050 have a lifestyle like Americans today, the capacity for the Earth to provide resources will be severely compromised.

Ecotourism in the Amazon rain forest

The dire consequences of climate change have galvanized millions of people adhering to a transformative worldview to work towards alternative and renewable energy, especially in the form of wind and solar energy. Our fossil fuel-dependent lifestyle has finally galvanized world-wide attention, even among some Western politicians, as a shift from our addiction to oil and coal is slowly underway. Events such as the first Earth Day in 1970, the Rio Environmental Conference in 1992, the Kyoto Treaty in 2001, the Copenhagen Climate Conference in 2009, and the United Nations Climate Change Conference in 2015 address the importance of a safe, healthy environment for sustainable human life. A growing number of people think it is of utmost importance to save the planet from environmental ravages.

A connected issue to energy, urban revitalization, is forcing many of us to rethink our car-dependent city configurations and accompanying suburban sprawl. Because of the excessive amounts of energy used to maintain this way of life, efforts are underway to switch to more energy efficient modes of public transportation. Also, the alienating nature of suburbs has sparked rethinking among some people to move to more community-focused neighborhoods that reduce commuting time and conserve valuable suburban land for agriculture and biodiversity.

Some ecologists suggest replacing the current economic measurement method—Gross Domestic Product (GDP), that merely measures national spending without regard to economic, environmental, or social well-being—with a **Genuine Progress Indicator** (GPI). The GPI, created by the organization Redefining Progress in 1995, measures the general economic and social well-being of all citizens. For example, if a business is responsible for an oil spill, the costs associated with the clean-up contribute to an increase in GDP, since the clean-up costs actually grow the economy according to this measurement. But GDP ignores environmental damage of the oil spill that has a negative long-lasting cost and impact. In calculating the GPI, the costs of the oil spill would be subtracted from the total, since it damages the environment over the long-term. When using GPI calculations, the U.S. economy has been stagnant since 1970.[7]

A growing number of ecologists see the Earth as an interconnected organism that awakens our sacred relationship with nature and positively supports our psychic well-being. This shift of consciousness revives an ancient mystical accord with nature that has sustained humans for millions of years. A modern worldview has contributed to a destructive relationship with the Earth. Some people feel that a more benign connection would improve human health and mental well-being as well as slow the extinction of many endangered species that add to the diversity of life.

Climate change

Even though we are overshooting Earth's carrying capacity, it is not too late to make changes. Our human capacity for thinking long-term, globally, and holistically does not have precedence, yet it is not beyond our capabilities. We can change, and we must do so. Adjusting our thinking to view the long-term consequences of our actions is paramount. Growth needs to be reconsidered as the mantra of our society; instead, practicing and acting within the limits of our Earth's capacity holds the key to our future well-being and survival.

CONCLUDING INSIGHTS:
THE TRANSFORMATIVE WORLDVIEW

The Global Wave poses a huge challenge for us—environmental degradation, a huge socio-economic gap, unchecked individualism, a political system out of touch with reality, and worldviews unable to deal with future challenges. Our innate behaviors and historical experiences have not prepared us well for the urgency of the global issues that confront us; we do not have a firm track record that we can draw on. Our innate behaviors as a species have equipped us to deal with a threat such as a marauding lion or the needs of our immediate 25 member group, but now we must deal with the threat of planet-wide environmental devastation and the needs of our immediate 7+ billion member group!

We often turn to our political or religious leaders as potential saviors. However, they are also overwhelmed with the issues or caught in their own intransigent, outdated worldview. Our political leaders in the U.S. are adept (somewhat) at dealing with isolated problems in a legally, deliberative, cumbersome way with built in mechanisms to stymie impulsive actions. But they have failed to provide a vision of where we need to head and what we need to do. With their enslavement to corporations for their campaign donations, their intransigent bi-partisanship, and their entrenched worldviews, many politicians are unable to provide the leadership the citizenry so desperately craves. The election in the U.S. of President Donald Trump in 2016 was a rejection of many liberal democratic principles that the country and Western nations have been founded upon. Half of the people in the

President Donald Trump, USA

U.S. voted for an authoritarian-type leader who is dispensing with checks and balances carefully put in place over the years and, instead, put their faith in a government run by wealthy oligarchs. Trump supporters are blithely rejecting our liberal traditions just to cut through the bureaucracy and get results that benefit them. These political actions, unprecedented in U.S. history, are sure to have profound consequences.

Some of our religious leaders have also failed us, although many are working hard to bring about change. Many religious people, for example, have scoffed at the idea of climate change, although some evangelical leaders are now alarmed that we humans are contaminating God's creation and are calling for action. Other religious people continue to disbelieve the hard scientific findings. They are embedded in the minutia of their faith and fail to see the "big picture" issues that are causing such distress around the world.

A challenge today and in the future is how to accommodate diverse opinions without losing social and national cohesiveness. There is a need to reduce the rigid dogma of fundamentalism without losing the sense of shared meaning and purpose that traditional religion offers. There is a need to embrace the technological wonders of the globalized worldview that connect people throughout the world, yet reject the rampant consumerism and social divide that economic globalization fosters. There is a need to counter the pessimism, obscurity, elitism, uninspiring and fragmenting effects of postmodern thought without losing the ability to probe below surface meanings. What worldview will emerge to replace the shattered worldviews that have failed to provide a framework that will enable us to address vast global problems?

Although some of the positive dimensions of the four worldviews have already been mentioned and need to be incorporated into the transformative worldview, each of the worldviews alone has glaring detriments harming our planet and undermining our future life. For example, for a more inclusive and culturally tolerant worldview we need to tone down the rigid dogma and intolerance of fundamentalism without losing the sense of shared meaning and universal values such as compassion and love that universal religions offer. We need to integrate the sense of local place and the consideration

Smiling !Kung girl, Africa, photo Izla Bardavid

of the environment that many traditional people have connected with for millennia without losing our awareness that we are all global citizens. We need to move beyond the mechanistic, segmented order of the modern worldview without losing the importance of scientific inquiry, secularism, rational, logical thought, and shared patriotism. We need to assimilate the advances in technology, transportation and communication, while rejecting the despoiling of our planet through environmental exploitation. The postmodern worldview of irrational behavior, bleakness, relative values, uncertainty, and pessimism is failing to inspire future generations. The obscurity, indeterminacy and elitism of postmodern and deconstructionist thought are providing unique perspectives about reality but do not provide enough inspiration for people to create a more just and sustainable future.

We need to counter the fragmenting, pessimistic, and uncertainty of postmodernism while incorporating the principles of relativity and the relationship of the observer and observed.

Some drawbacks to the transformative worldview are that many enthusiasts feel self-righteous about their "cause" and are unwilling to listen to others. The sanctimonious behavior among some has estranged many people who otherwise might be drawn to the worthy causes. While shouting tolerance and rejection of hate, many have shown intolerance to views other than their own, especially on college campuses. Hardly a movement that is inclusive! A willingness to listen and consider other views and people will do much to further many of the positive qualities of the transformative worldview and the dedicated people advancing its initiatives.

Those supporting a transformative worldview need not totally disregard the other four worldviews in shaping a new one, yet they need to be selective and mindful in fitting values of the other worldviews into a new framework. Even though the traditional, modern, and globalized worldviews are currently the dominant paradigms at this point in time, the transformative worldview is gaining momentum and continues to mount a vigorous challenge to mainstream ideas while offering viable options for a sustainable and more equitable future. Which worldview or combination of worldviews will global citizens choose for our future? While some people are already taking action, others are going through a process of debate, consideration, and deliberation. We all have a voice and critical stake in the future outcome.

Transcending worldviews

The modern and globalized worldviews, the dominant views currently, are, in my opinion, incapable of addressing the challenges we face. In fact, they exacerbate the problems! Paradoxically, the competitive individualistic behaviors that served us in the modern worldview are the opposite behaviors we need to deal with problems such as climate change and rising inequality. This problem requires collective action, long-term commitment, and cooperation among diverse people, while giving up our addiction to immediate self-gratification and short-term solutions. The reward—saving our planet for future generations—is well worth any sacrifices we may have to make. Unfortunately, that goal seems too remote and disconnected from the everyday lives of many people who have immediate concerns such as having enough food to put on the table. For many people, the transition to a new way of thinking and acting is a difficult transition to make. But many people are inspired to make the world livable and safe for our children and grandchildren. Although we eagerly install fluorescent light bulbs or turn off our computers at night, deep structural, systemic changes are difficult to accomplish on our own. Our worldviews are embedded in the way society is structured; it is hard to make the leap to another worldview. Writers have written of a "tipping point," where things quickly make a dramatic shift to something different. The signals that we need to shift to a different worldview are becoming ever more readily apparent. The leap to a transformative worldview is ever more urgent.

The Transformative Worldview

It is urgent to create a different worldview that can enable us to avert environmental collapse, deal with the myriad of issues facing us today and in the near future, and forge a way of life that is happier and more fulfilling. Inspired by these goals, I have written this book from a transformative worldview perspective, promoting it as a viable worldview today and in the future. After much research and reflection, I find that transformation is necessary to help us make the shift to a new way of thinking and acting that will move us into a new and more creative, tolerant, compassionate, and sustainable relationship with each other and our world.

One step in formulating and expanding a transformative worldview is one that you have just accomplished: reading about different worldviews and imagining and practicing how to interact with other people holding different worldviews. My goal is not for us to forcibly convert people to a transformative worldview, but through listening, kindness, and compassionate conversations we can actively demonstrate to others that the transformative worldview is a life-enhancing future scenario in which all people have a crucial stake. It is my intent and hope that through engaging with others and seeing other perspectives, we can shift our consciousness to a transformative worldview. We can make that leap!

Afterword

An Emerging Worldview: The Populist Worldview

A new worldview is emerging! As I was wrapping up this book for publication, I felt that I was omitting a significant worldview that is sweeping the United States and Europe: A populist worldview. After all, it is a movement that elected a president in the United States, Donald Trump, made in-roads into Europe, and has sparked raw emotions among such a large group of people that it should not be ignored. Donald Trump and his followers don't fit into any of the five worldviews very neatly. Perhaps he needs his own worldview category. It is still unclear, at the time of this writing, if it will emerge into a full-scale worldview or recede from public awareness without accomplishing its agenda.

I am calling this emerging worldview a populist worldview. From all indicators, it is gaining steam in the U.S. with the election of Trump, in the United Kingdom with the pro-Brexit vote, in France with the popularity of the National Front's Marine Le Pen, and other European countries. I will mainly concentrate on the Trump phenomenon in the U.S., while noting that his agenda is not being carried out in isolation but follows similar patterns emerging throughout the world.

U.S. President Donald Trump

First of all, I would like to give some context to this populist worldview. Since the 1980s, the U.S. has led a globalization agenda guided by neoliberal principles. Economic globalization in particular has spread quickly around the world. This globalization/neoliberal process has been characterized by four major shifts in the U.S.: 1) many national corporations sent their operations to low-wage countries to increase profit margins, 2) the government, with corporate blessings, loosened immigration quotas or ignored illegal immigration in order to have a supply of cheap labor at home and a bulwark against unions, 3) rapid technological changes created greater efficiencies in the workplace that have eliminated many jobs and disrupted everyday life, and 4) the changing nature of the nation-state and patriotism influenced by the influx of immigrants and an allegiance by the global elite/educated class to a global rather than local/national agenda.

The results from these four major shifts have been: 1) historic levels of income inequality and concentration of wealth at the very top, 2) technological advancements that have been celebrated by Silicon Valley but have disrupted jobs and the social fabric, 3) a shrinking middle/working class who have experienced stagnant wages and fewer opportunities, 4) a disruption of shared, core values revolving around a shared love of country and a fraying of the social fabric (social institutions) that binds the country together.

These four global forces have hit all of us in many ways, but arguably the group hit the hardest in the U.S. is the working class and poor who don't hold a college education. Their wages have stagnated for decades and opportunities for well-paying jobs with non-technical skills have also declined. These four forces have occurred in many core countries (Western, industrialized countries)

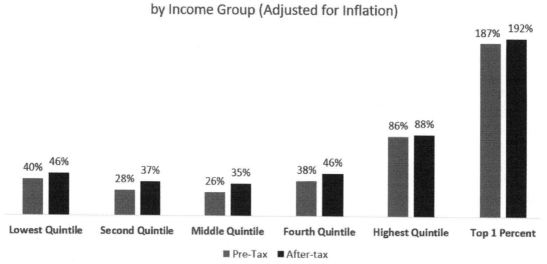

U.S. Income: Percent Change Comparing 1979 and 2013 by Income Group (Adjusted for Inflation)

Source Data: CBO "The Distribution of Household Income and Federal Taxes, 2013" Supplemental Data

in Europe with similar results. As the middle class grows in Asian countries and other emerging economies, the middle class in core countries is shrinking.

The frustration of this group has been building for years, and in the 2016 presidential election it was directed at the political class for ignoring their plight. The Democratic Party, long a champion of the working class, has turned to the globalizers and technocrats as core constituents, and

Democratic Party logo

hasn't found a way to blend the working class (especially whites') agenda into their platform of contending constituents: The young, immigrants, people of color, LGBT, urban, and college-educated. With their embrace of immigration, even illegal immigration, the left has angered this working class group that has experienced competition from these low-wage workers for a shrinking pool of manufacturing and well-paying but low skill jobs. As indicated from the 2016 presidential election results, apparently the needs of the left's disparate coalition of groups didn't resonate with the needs of the working class.

The Republican Party, long the party of the globalizers, has also melded a diverse constituency into a tension-filled party. Their core group, evangelicals, holds the party together despite the fact that Republicans haven't implemented much of their agenda. The Reagan Democrats, many of the white working-class who switched to the Republicans with the Reagan election in 1980, often switch back and forth between the two parties depending on the candidate and agenda.

Over the last few decades, I have found that the political parties in the U.S. have drawn a line with a permanent marker between their ideologies. If any Democrats, for example, deviate from the "established" stances on same-sex marriage, abortion, health care, immigration, trade, taxes, foreign policy, or a host of other issues, then their constituents spring into action to condemn their views. The same holds true for Republicans. Even though both parties share

Republican Party logo

similar views on a globalized economy and appeasing the corporate world, grid-lock still results.

With all these bubbling tensions simmering in a cauldron, along came the 2016 presidential election. In early 2016, no one would have imagined that the forces of globalization would be challenged from both the left and right. The populist worldview was taking shape. I believe there will emerge two factions to the populist worldview: The left and the right, each trying to hone the issues that will define this worldview. The Democratic and Republican parties of old will cease to exist as in the past several decades and will be shaped anew.

On the left, and arguably also part of the populist movement, was the Democratic candidacy of Bernie Sanders. Sanders attacked Hillary Clinton, the eventual Democratic nominee, where it hurt: On her globalization policies—trade and outsourcing—that have contributed to greater income inequality and pain for the working and middle classes. To many people, she seemed too adjoined to corporate America, which was blamed for all ailments of American society. The two candidates seemed to agree on other policies such as immigration, identity politics, catering to the youth vote, and social issues. Sanders drilled down hard on the

Bernie Sanders at Rutgers University

inequality issue and it especially resonated with the college-educated youth, who saw shrinking opportunities ahead of them while tethered to student debt.

On the right, along came Trump. He was different, both ideologically and emotionally, from the other Republican candidates. He pledged to smash through the ideological divide and to "Make America Great Again." It sounded good and enough people believed him to catapult him to the highest office in the land, despite his crass outbursts and lack of experience.

In forming a populist worldview, Trump has borrowed aspects from the other worldviews and invented some new characteristics. He has borrowed the tribal notion (see indigenous worldview) of loyalty to family and to a very few of his closest advisers. He is fiercely loyal to the family business, and doesn't entrust its operations to anyone outside his inner circle. He regards his family members, especially his daughter Ivanka and her husband, as heirs to his fortune and political empire.

During the modern worldview, there was a fierce division between two political approaches in the 20th century: Authoritarian rule and liberal democracy. This confrontation came to a head during World War II when the authoritarian governments of Germany and Italy (fascists) fought the liberal democracies of the U.S., Britain, parts of France, and also the authoritarian communist regime of the Soviet Union

Trump's administration has not, in my opinion, crossed the line to fascism but many of his policies and actions are uncomfortably close to that ideology. Fascism is a complete rejection of liberal democracy. Trump seems intent on dismantling the levers of liberalism and the checks and balances on

Mussolini and Hitler

his power. The populist worldview is essentially undemocratic, a characteristic that doesn't seem to be that egregious among populists. Trump derides the press at every instance; a sure way to try to discredit those who check his power. His latent fascist tendencies should be carefully monitored.

During his campaign, Trump railed against free trade agreements—the cornerstone of the globalized worldview—that he claimed hurt American workers. He has nixed the Trans-Pacific Free Trade Agreement with Asian counterparts. On occasion he chastises American corporations planning to send jobs to Mexico or overseas. Populists want an end to free trade agreements such as

NAFTA and a return to bilateral trade negotiations. They are in favor of levying a tariff on goods imported into the U.S. from American firms manufacturing in countries who have taken advantage of low-wage foreign labor. However, it will take a lot more than these token efforts to fulfill the promise he made to American workers that their jobs would return to American soil.

Even though Trump rejects some aspects of the globalized worldview, he is supportive of others, such as perpetuating oligarchical rule by appointing billionaires to his cabinet.

NAFTA logo

Many voters hailed his business experience as a reason for voting for him. They want an end to regulations and for the economy to grow, and grow fast. Trump is also intent on enacting globalization/neoliberal staples such as lowering taxes for the wealthy, removing "burdensome" regulations, privatizing public assets such as education, and many others.

Globalizers, both Republicans and Democrats, have been very supportive of immigration for the last several decades. Immigration has added many pluses to American society by making it more diverse and, in my opinion, more interesting. But the influx of immigrants has also helped the globalization agenda by providing cheap labor for its enterprises and attracting the brightest workers from around the world to the tech industry in Silicon Valley. Trump has sworn to stop illegal immigration. Populists cheer when Trump brags about building a wall to further separate Mexico and the U.S., spending upwards of billions of dollars for this effort. They want to curtail if not eliminate immigration and "round-up" immigrants who are in the U.S. illegally, especially if they have a criminal record. This means approximately 11 million illegal immigrants, probably a number too large and costly for deportation efforts. However, his ill-conceived orders have created more chaos and fostered more ill-will than necessary. Although the immigration issue has been passed on down the line by Democrats and Republicans for too long, Trump's policies are problematic.

Border wall with Mexico

Some of the policies advocated by the populist agenda may seem reasonable and within the bounds of the Constitution. However, the implementation of the populist agenda by Trump is a problem. His constant and blatant lies, unstable rantings, gloomy future scenarios, and unwarranted attacks on the press are unacceptable to the majority of Americans and a threat to democracy. He has anemic policies, if any, and no idea how to channel these policies into actual laws. He seems to govern by tweeting with little thought as to the consequences of his actions. The executive branch of the government is supposed to execute the laws, under Trump this is absent.

The wall provides an apt metaphor for the populist worldview. Trump and his supporters want to wall themselves off from the rest of the world by embracing a nationalistic, isolationist foreign policy agenda. They want to wall themselves off from outsiders, the out-group, while protecting the loyal in-group. They want to wall themselves off from democratic institutions such as a free press, constitutional guidelines, and etiquette, manners, and what has been traditionally considered "decent" behavior by mainstream society. Practically every day a new wall is being "built," dividing our nation from the traditions, customs, and laws of the past; tearing at an already tattered social fabric holding the nation together by just a few threads.

The good news is that the U.S. is a well-established liberal democracy with long-standing institutions run by committed people. We have withstood deep divisions through history—slavery, the Civil War, Reconstruction, the Depression, World War II, the 1968 rebellions—that could have easily torn apart a country with less sound institutions. It is up to these institutions—the judicial

branch, press, civic institutions, local/state governments, empowered ordinary citizens, and others—to help us weather the negative aspects of the populist storm that seems bent on disrupting more than building, excluding rather than including, and hating more than kindness.

Will this populist worldview become the dominant worldview during this time that I call the Global Wave? Will enough people embrace this worldview, creating a tipping point in which it begins to holistically affect all the technological, social, political, economic, and religious patterns in our society? We can hope that if the populist worldview becomes more understood and the policies become more defined that enough people will say, "This is not what we had in mind; I want no part of it." Working with others resisting this worldview and building a transformative worldview seems to me very important at this time in our history. We all have a stake in the outcome.

The Global Wave: Five Worldviews

Worldview	Indigenous	Modern	Fundamentalist	Globalized	Transformative
Values and Beliefs	connections nature's ways intangible continuity cyclical very slow live out	individualism competition certainty tangible Newtonian machine separation, categories division, compartments stages of development predictable, orderly chronological, linear	divine certainty, inspiration, moral certitude, unquestioning, dogma, creed, concrete representation, absolute, irreducible, literal, exact, devout, strident	individualism, scientific inquiry, Einstein relativity, uncertainty, irrational, competition, struggle, instantaneous, fragmented, opportunity, warp speed	interdependence, limits to science, organic possibility, imagination, systems thinking, holistic, compassion, collective, deliberative, contemplative, understanding, support, complementarity, synergy, process, integration, cyclical
Political Views	tribal wars, conflict scarce resource, tribal governing/councils, elders' wisdom, mediation	private ownership, nation-state, liberalism, socialism, communism, conquest, warfare, punishment, struggle	conservative, prescribed order, hierarchical, theocracy, deference to authority, battle unbelievers, punishment, discipline	corporate influence, warfare scarce resources, dollar democracy, intellectual property, "underachievers," short-term thinking	participatory democracy, community networks, self-organizing, defensive conflict, conflict scarce resources, dialogue
Economic Views	reciprocity, redistribution, local trade & distribution, domestic economy	capitalism (mercantilism, classical, regulated), socialism/communism, economic growth, mass production	market fundamentalism, market is the "god," neoliberalism, economic growth	neoliberal capitalism, state capitalism, privatization, patents, commodification, hyper consumerism, economic growth	mixed economy, public ownership/commons, domestic economy, worker owned cooperatives, local agriculture & businesses, non-profit sector
Cultural Views	traditional wisdom, folk religions, animistic, ancestor worship	scientific method, reason, logic, reducible, faith in science, progress, secular, rational religion	faith in revealed truth, holy book authority, belief in science if not in conflict with divine truths, religious exclusivity	religion irrelevant, cutthroat competition, commodification of culture, social relations	spiritual, inclusive religious groups, multi-cultural, faith in people, collective, unity within diversity
Environmental Views	nature alive, natural rhythms, faith in nature, rooted in place	nature inanimate, exploit nature as commodity, nature limitless	nature is God's dominion, nature subdued for humans, nature is God's creation, humans preserve it	nature commodity, conflict scarce resources, environmental limits	sustainability, nature animate, earth-based connection, nature's limits
Social Views	customs/traditions, egalitarian, kinship bonds relationship, community, elders' wisdom, exclusivity, local group, local history	intolerant "other," nuclear family, racism, social classes, hierarchy, patriarchy, mass education, national history	theocracy, patriarchy, hierarchy, own religious tribe, religious education, history based on religious beliefs, tenets	nuclear family, consumption family, privatized education, education for global competition	relationships, inclusive networks, reinvention of family, global community, holistic education, holistic world history

Comparative Thought: Five Worldviews

Indigenous Worldview	Modern Worldview	Fundamentalist Worldview	Globalized Worldview	Transformative Worldview
nature	scientific method	holy book authority	scientific inquiry	limits to science
nature's ways	Newtonian machine	divine certainty	Einstein relativity	Einstein relativity
natural rhythms	certainty	moral certitude	uncertainty	possibility
faith in nature	faith in science	faith in revealed truth	faith in markets	faith in people
traditional wisdom	scientific certainty	divinely inspired	theory of relativity	systems thinking
tradition	progress	unquestioning	irrational	unity within diversity
stream	reason, logic	dogma	probable knowledge	consciousness
flow	mechanistic	unchanging	approximations	interdependence
flux	autonomous, separate	consistent	instantaneous	simultaneity
the group	individualism	religious community	individualism	global community
connections	scientific determinism	prescribed order	tendencies	imagination
community	stages of development	hierarchical structure	fragmented	holistic
flows	compartmentalization	divisions	opportunity	networks
exclusivity of group	intolerant "other"	religious exclusivity	class exclusivity	inclusive
passive	competition	strident	comparative advantage	relationship
emotional	rational, reason	passion	discontinuous	compassion, emotion
live out	predictability	concrete	contradictory	process, integration
ambiguity	reducible	irreducible	uncertainty	relativity
changelessness	objective thinking	absolute	subjective thinking	understanding
very slow	expedient	slow	warped speed	deliberate, contemplative

Comparative Thought: Five Worldviews

folk religion, animistic	rational religion (deism)	universal religions	question religion	spiritual
customs, traditions	secular	devout	nonrepresentational	earth-based connections
intangible	tangible	literal	abstract	organic
nature alive	nature inanimate	nature subdued	nature commodity	nature alive
extended family	nuclear family	religious family	consumption family	community networks
egalitarian	order, hierarchy	unchanging order	arbitrary	complementarity
continuity	change	continuity	change, random	self-organizing
kinship bonds	racial discrimination	religious discrimination	class separation	multi-cultural
reciprocity	economic growth	modern economy	hyper economic growth	sustainability
story	debate	sermon	discussion	dialogue
harmony	conquest	religious conversion	market conversion	synergy
group democracy	liberalism	theocracy	elite democracy	participatory democracy
tribal wars	war for conquest	religious war	terrorism	defensive conflict
conflict over scarcity	struggle, conflict, war	battle unbelievers	cutthroat competition	conflict scarce resources
cyclical	chronological, linear	teleological	indeterminacy	comparative, cyclical
community	ownership	religious wealth	privatization	collective
hand-crafted	mass-production	household economy	efficiency, growth	community economy
ban from group	punish non-conformity	punishment evildoers	punish underachievers	support, nourish
learn from nature	mass education	religious education	privatized education	holistic education

Endnotes

Chapter 1: Introduction to Worldviews: The Way We See the World

1 "Who should own Native American artifacts?" *Annenberg Classroom*, ret. 8/16/16. http://www.annenbergclassroom.org/speakouts.aspx?name=who-should-own-native-american-artifacts&AspxAutoDetectCookieSupport=1

2 Donella & Dennis Meadows, Jorgen Randers, *Limits to Growth: The Thirty Year Update* (White River Junction, Vermont: Chelsea Green Publishing Company, 2004) 4.

3 Emmanuel Wallerstein, "Introductory Essay to Essential Wallerstein," *Yale University Faculty Page.*

4 John Goekler, "Teaching for the Future: Systems Thinking and Sustainability," *Green Teacher 70*, (Spring 2003) 8-14.

5 Michelle LeBaron, "Cultural and Worldview Frames," *Knowledge Based Essay*, (August 2003). http://www.beyondintractability.org/essay/cultural_frames/

6 "Indigenous Peoples and the United Nations System," *United Nations, Office of the High Commissioner for Human Rights, United Nations Office at Geneva,* ret. 9/09. http://www.unhchr.ch/html/racism/indileaflet1.doc.> and "Indigenous issues," *International Work Group on Indigenous Affairs,* ret. 9/09. http://www.iwgia.org/sw155.asp>. The 5% is based on a population of 7 billion people

7 LeBaron, "Cultural and Worldview Frames," *Knowledge Based Essay.*

8 LeBaron, "Cultural and Worldview Frames," *Knowledge Based Essay.*

9 LeBaron, "Cultural and Worldview Frames," *Knowledge Based Essay.*

10 LeBaron, "Cultural and Worldview Frames," *Knowledge Based Essay.*

Chapter 2. The Indigenous Worldview

1 "Peoples of the World," *National Geographic Society.*

2 "United Nations Declaration on the Rights of Indigenous Peoples," *United Nations UNPFII.* http://www.un.org/esa/socdev/unpfii/documents/DRIPS_en.pdf

3 "Indigenous Peoples and the United Nations System," *Office of the High Commissioner for Human Rights, United Nations Office at Geneva.* http://www.unhchr.ch/html/racism/indileaflet1.doc and "Indigenous Issues," *International Work Group on Indigenous Affairs.* http://www.iwgia.org/sw155.asp

4 *The United Nations.* http://www.un.org/

5 "Indigenous Peoples, Indigenous Voices," *United Nations Permanent Forum on Indigenous Issues*, ret. 5/20/16. http://www.un.org/esa/socdev/unpfii/documents/5session_factsheet1.pdf

6 Courtney Carver, "Story of the Mexican Fisherman," *Be More With Less*, ret. 8/19/16. http://bemorewithless.com/the-story-of-the-mexican-fisherman/

7 "Collective property in South America, challenges and prospects," *LandPortal.info*, ret. 12/8/16. https://landportal.info/debates/2016/collective-property-south-america-challenges-and-prospects

8 Rigoberta Menchu, (trans. Ann Wright), *I, Rigoberta Menchu: An Indian Woman in Guatemala*, (New York: Verso Press, 1984) 2.

9 Menchu *I, Rigoberta Menchu*, 134.

10 Menchu *I, Rigoberta Menchu*, 24-25.

11 "Indigenous Peoples, Indigenous Voices," *United Nations Permanent Forum on Indigenous Issues*, ret. 5/20/16. http://www.un.org/esa/socdev/unpfii/documents/5session_factsheet1.pdf

12 "Indigenous Peoples, Indigenous Voices," *United Nations.*

Chapter 3: The Modern Worldview

1 Gerhard and Jean Lenski, *Human Societies: An Introduction to Macrosociology,* (New York: McGraw-Hill, 1982) 341.

2 Lenski, *Human Societies*, 342-344.

3 Peter N. Stearns, *World History: Patterns of Change and Continuity*, (New York: Harper Collins Publishers, 1995) 300.

4 Lenski, *Human Societies*, 342-344.

5 Norman F. Kantor, *The American Century: Varieties of Culture in Modern Times,* (New York: Harper Perennial, 1997) 425-431.

6 Kantor, *American Century*, 454-455.

Chapter 4: The Fundamentalist Worldview

1   Benjamin Beit-Hallahmi, "Fundamentalism," *Global Policy Forum*, (May 2000).
2   "Secular Fundamentalism," *New York Times Opinion*, (December, 19, 2003). http://www.nytimes.com/2003/12/19/opinion/19iht-edscarf_ed3_.html
3   Peter Huff, "Parallels in Muslim, Christian, and Jewish, and Christian Fundamentalism," *World and I.* http://www.worldandi.com/subscribers/feature_detail.asp?num=24175
4   Karen Armstrong, *The Case for God*, (New York: Alfred A. Knopf, 2009) 271.
5   Armstrong, *Case for God*, 235.
6   Armstrong, *Case for God*, 236-238.
7   Armstrong, *Case for God*, 236-238.
8   Armstrong, *Case for God*, 238.
9   Armstrong, *Case for God*, 239.
10 Armstrong, *Case for God*, 247-249.
11 Armstrong, *Case for God*, 249 and 254.
12 Armstrong, *Case for God*, 269-270.
13 Armstrong, *Case for God*, 270.
14 Armstrong, *Case for God*, 271.
15 Armstrong, *Case for God*, 272-273.
16 Armstrong, *Case for God*, 273.
17 Armstrong, *Case for God*, 274.
18 Armstrong, *Case for God*, 275.
19 Armstrong, *Case for God*, 293-294.
20 Armstrong, *Case for God*, 292.
21 Armstrong, *Case for God*, 295.
22 Armstrong, *Case for God*, 295.
23 Armstrong, *Case for God*, 293-294 and 299.
24 Armstrong, *Case for God*, 296.
25 Armstrong, *Case for God*, 296-297.
26 Armstrong, *Case for God*, 297.
27 Armstrong, *Case for God*, 297.
28 Armstrong, *Case for God*, 298.
29 Armstrong, *Case for God*, 299
30 Armstrong, *Case for God*, 293-294
31 Armstrong, *Case for God*, 293.

Chapter 5: The Globalized Worldview

1   Ian Bremmer, *The End of the Free Market: Who Wins the War Between States and Corporations?* (New York: Portfolio, 2010) 33 and 40.
2   Bremmer, *Free Market*, cover jacket, 21 and 42.
3   Walden Bello, "The Global Financial System in Crisis," *Speech at People's Development Forum*, University of the Philippines (Mar. 25, 2008). http://www.waldenbello.org/index2.php?option=com_content&task=view&id=86&pop=1&page
4   Walden Bello, "A Primer on the Wall Street Meltdown," *Focus on the Global South* (2008). http://www.waldenbello.org/index2.php?option=com_content&task=view&id=98&pop=1&page
5   Madeline Levine, "Challenging the Culture of Affluence," *Independent School* (2007) 28-36. http://www.nais.org/publications/ismagazinearticle.cfm?ItemNumber=150274
6   Benjamin R. Barber, *Consumed: How Markets Corrupt Children, Infantilize Adults, and Swallow Citizens Whole* (New York: Norton & Co., 2007).
7   Barber, *Consumed*, 167.
8   Robert Costanza, "Toward a new Sustainable Economy," *Real World Economics Review* (Mar. 26, 2009) 1, in *Common Dreams*.org. www.commondreams.org/print/40015
9   James Gustave Speth, *The Bridge at the Edge of the World: Capitalism, the Environment, and Crossing from Crisis to Sustainability* (New Haven: Yale University Press, 2008) 46-47.
10 Donella & Dennis Meadows, Jorgen Randers, *Limits to Growth: The Thirty Year Update* (White River Junction, Vermont: Chelsea Green Publishing Company, 2004) 6.
11 Martin Carnoy, Manuel Castells, Stephen S. Cohen, Fernando Henrique Carduso, *The New Global Economy in the*

Information Age: Reflections on our Changing World (University Park, PA: The Pennsylvania State University Press, 1993) 1-3 and 5-6 and Michael Perelman, *Class Warfare in the Information Age* (New York: St. Martin's Press, 1998) 16.

[12] "Uber May be Worth $50 billion. Really?" *CNN Money*, (July 8, 2015), ret. 7/8/15. http://money.cnn. com/2015/05/11/investing/uber-50-billion-valuation/index.html

[13] "Economics," *About.com.* http://economics.about.com/od/economicsglossary/g/stolper.htm and Thomas Palley, "Labor Threat," *Tom Paine* (Oct, 4, 2005) 1. www.zmag.org/content/print_articles.cfm?itemID=8867&section ID=1

[14] Thomas Palley, "Labor Threat." *Tom Paine* (Oct. 4, 2005) 1. http://www.zmag.org/content/print_article. cfm?itemID=8867&sectionID=1

[15] Samuelson quoted in Palley, "Labor Threat," *Tom Paine,* 2.

[16] Nayan Chanda, *Bound Together: How Traders, Preachers, Warriors, Adventurers and Warriors Shaped Globalization,* (New York: Caravan Books, 2007) 294.

[17] Don Peck, "Can the Middle Class be Saved," *The Atlantic* (Sept. 2011) 63. http://www.theatlantic.com/magazine/ print/2011/09/can-the-middle-class-be-saved/8600

[18] Joseph E. Stiglitz, "Of the 1%, for the 1%, by the 1%," *Vanity Fair* (May 2011). http://www.vanityfair.com/society/ features/2011/05/top-one-percent-201105

[19] Jon Jeter, *Flat broke in the free market* (New York: W.W. Norton & Co., 2009) xiii.

[20] Sam Pizzigati, "Mapping Global Wealth," *OtherWords.* http://otherwords.org/mapping_global_wealth/

[21] Jeter, *Flat Broke,* xiii.

[22] Barber, *Consumed,* 102.

Chapter 6: The Transformative Worldview

[1] Fritjof Capra, *The Turning Point: Science, Society, and the Rising Culture* (Toronto: Bantam Books, 1982) 21-53.

[2] Norman F. Kantor, *American Century: Varieties of Culture in Modern Times,* (New York: HarperCollins Publishers, 1997) 425-431.

[3] Farouk Mawlawi, "New Conflicts, New Challenges: The Evolving Role for Non-Governmental Actors," *Journal of International Affairs* (Winter 1993) 392.

[4] Mary E. Clark, *Ariadne's Thread: The Search for New Modes of Thinking* (New York: St. Martin's Press, 1989) 490-492.

[5] Wendell Berry, "Decolonizing Rural America," *Audubon* (Vol. 95, No. 2, March-April, 1993) 105.

[6] Gar Alperovitz, "America Beyond Capitalism," *Dollars & Sense* (2011).

[7] "Genuine Progress Indicator," *Redefining Progress.* http://www.rprogress.org/sustainability_indicators/genuine_ progress_indicator.htm

[8] Fritjof Capra, *The Turning Point,* 21-53.

[9] Norman F. Kantor, *American Century: Varieties of Culture in Modern Times,* (New York: HarperCollins Publishers, 1997), 425-431.

[10] Farouk Mawlawi, "New Conflicts, New Challenges: The Evolving Role for Non-Governmental Actors," *Journal of International Affairs* (Winter 1993) 392.

[11] Mary E. Clark, *Ariadne's Thread,* 490-492.

[12] Wendell Berry, "Decolonizing Rural America," *Audubon* (Vol. 95, No. 2, March-April, 1993) 105.

[13] Alperovitz, "America Beyond Capitalism," *Dollars & Sense.*

[14] "Genuine Progress Indicator," *Redefining Progress.*

Bibliography

About.com. "Economics." http://economics.about.com/od/economicsglossary/g/stolper.htm

Alperovitz, Gar. "America Beyond Capitalism," *Dollars & Sense,* (2011).

Annenberg Classroom. "Who should own Native American artifacts?" ret. 8/16/16.
   http://www.annenbergclassroom.org/speakouts.aspx?name=who-should-own-native-american-
   artifacts&AspxAutoDetectCookieSupport=1

Armstrong, Karen. *The Case for God,* (New York: Alfred A. Knopf, 2009).

Barber, Benjamin R. *Consumed: How Markets Corrupt Children, Infantilize Adults, and Swallow Citizens Whole,* (New
   York: Norton & Co., 2007).

Beit-Hallahmi, Benjamin. "Fundamentalism," *Global Policy Forum,* (May 2000).

Bello, Walden. "A Primer on the Wall Street Meltdown," *Focus on the Global South,* (2008).
   http://www.waldenbello.org/index2.php?option=com_content&task=view&id=98&pop=1&page

Bello, Walden. "The Global Financial System in Crisis," *Speech at People's Development Forum,* University of the
   Philippines (Mar. 25, 2008). http://www.waldenbello.org/index2.php?option=com_content&task=view&id=86&
   pop=1&page

Berry, Wendell. "Decolonizing Rural America," *Audubon,* (Vol. 95, No. 2, March-April, 1993).

Bremmer, Ian. *The End of the Free Market: Who Wins the War Between States and Corporations?* (New York: Portfolio,
   2010).

Capra, Fritjof. *The Turning Point: Science, Society, and the Rising Culture,* (Toronto: Bantam Books, 1982).

Carnoy, Martin, Castells, Manuel, Cohen, Stephen S., Carduso, Fernando Henrique. *The New Global Economy in the
   Information Age: Reflections on our Changing World,* (University Park, PA: The Pennsylvania State University Press,
   1993).

Carver, Courtney. "Fisherman Story," *Be More With Less,* ret. 8/19/16. http://bemorewithless.com/the-story-of-the-
   mexican-fisherman/

Chanda, Nayan. *Bound Together: How Traders, Preachers, Warriors, Adventurers and Warriors Shaped Globalization,*
   (New York: Caravan Books, 2007).

Clark, Mary E. *Ariadne's Thread: The Search for New Modes of Thinking,* (New York: St. Martin's Press, 1989).

CNN Money. "Uber May be Worth $50 billion. Really?" (July 8, 2015), ret. 7/8/15.
   http://money.cnn.com/2015/05/11/investing/uber-50-billion-valuation/index.html

Costanza, Robert. "Toward a new Sustainable Economy," *Real World Economics Review* (Mar. 26, 2009), in *Common
   Dreams*.org. www.commondreams.org/print/40015

Goekler, John. "Teaching for the Future: Systems Thinking and Sustainability," *Green Teacher 70,* (Spring 2003, 8-
   14).

Huff, Peter. "Parallels in Muslim, Christian, and Jewish, and Christian Fundamentalism," *World and I.*
   http://www.worldandi.com/subscribers/feature_detail.asp?num=24175

International Work Group on Indigenous Affairs. "Indigenous issues." http://www.iwgia.org/sw155.asp

Jeter, Jon. *Flat broke in the free market,* (New York: W.W. Norton & Co., 2009).

Kantor, Norman F. *The American Century: Varieties of Culture in Modern Times,* (New York: Harper Perennial, 1997).

LandPortal.info. "Collective property in South America, challenges and prospects," ret. 12/8/16.
   https://landportal.info/debates/2016/collective-property-south-america-challenges-and-prospects

LeBaron, Michelle. "Cultural and Worldview Frames," *Knowledge Based Essay,* (August 2003).
   http://www.beyondintractability.org/essay/cultural_frames/

Lenski, Gerhard and Lenski, Jean. *Human Societies: An Introduction to Macrosociology,* (New York: McGraw-Hill, 1982).

Levine, Madeline. "Challenging the Culture of Affluence," *Independent School*, (2007). http://www.nais.org/publications/ismagazinearticle.cfm?ItemNumber=150274

Mawlawi, Farouk. "New Conflicts, New Challenges: The Evolving Role for Non-Governmental Actors," *Journal of International Affairs* (Winter 1993).

Meadows, Donella & Dennis, Randers, Jorgen. *Limits to Growth: The Thirty Year Update,* (White River Junction, Vermont: Chelsea Green Publishing Company, 2004).

Menchu, Rigoberta. (trans. Ann Wright), *I, Rigoberta Menchu: An Indian Woman in Guatemala,* (New York: Verso Press, 1984).

National Geographic Society. "Peoples of the World."

New York Times Opinion, December, 19, 2003. http://www.nytimes.com/2003/12/19/opinion/19iht-edscarf_ed3_.html

Palley, Thomas. "Labor Threat," *Tom Paine,* (Oct, 4, 2005). zmag.org/content/print_articles.cfm?itemID=8867 &section ID=1

Peck, Don. "Can the Middle Class be Saved," *The Atlantic* (Sept. 2011). http://www.theatlantic.com/magazine/print/2011/09/can-the-middle-class-be-saved/8600

Perelman, Michael. *Class Warfare in the Information Age,* (New York: St. Martin's Press, 1998).

Pizzigati, Sam."Mapping Global Wealth," *OtherWords.* http://otherwords.org/mapping_global_wealth/ *Redefining Progress,* "Genuine Progress Indicator." http://www.rprogress.org/sustainability_indicators/genuine_progress_indicator.htm

Speth, James Gustave. *The Bridge at the Edge of the World: Capitalism, the Environment, and Crossing from Crisis to Sustainability,* (New Haven: Yale University Press, 2008).

Stearns, Peter N., *World History: Patterns of Change and Continuity*, (New York: Harper Collins Publishers, 1995).

Stiglitz, Joseph E. "Of the 1%, for the 1%, by the 1%," *Vanity Fair* (May 2011). http://www.vanityfair.com/society/features/2011/05/top-one-percent-201105

United Nations, International Work Group on Indigenous Affairs. "Indigenous issues," ret. 9/09. http://www.iwgia.org/sw155.asp

United Nations, Office of the High Commissioner for Human Rights. "Indigenous Peoples and the United Nations System," ret. 9/09. http://www.unhchr.ch/html/racism/indileaflet1.doc

United Nations Permanent Forum on Indigenous Issues. "Indigenous Peoples, Indigenous Voices," ret. 5/20/16. http://www.un.org/esa/socdev/unpfii/documents/5session_factsheet1.pdf

United Nations UNPFII. "United Nations Declaration on the Rights of Indigenous Peoples," http://www.un.org/esa/socdev/unpfii/documents/DRIPS_en.pdf

Wallerstein, Emmanuel, "Introductory Essay to Essential_Wallerstein, *Yale University Faculty Page.*

Glossary

alienation is the state in which people feel separated or detached from their past experiences or their family or group. (2)

Bryan, William Jennings (1860-1925) launched a crusade against evolution in school and colleges. He put Darwinism at the forefront of the fundamentalist agenda. (4)

capitalism an economic system in which private parties make their goods and services available in an open market and seek to make a profit on their activities. Private parties own the means of production. Two variations of capitalism: free market capitalism, often called *laissez faire*, and managed or regulated capitalism. (3)

communism a theory or system of social organization based on the holding of all property in common with actual ownership held by the state. The Soviet Union, the first communist nation, was formed in 1917, when a revolution led by Vladimir Lenin overthrew the Russian monarchy. The Soviet Union continued as a communist form of government until its collapse in 1991. (3)

Darwin, Charles (1809-1882) theorized that humans were not divinely created, as the Christian world had confidentially assumed for centuries, but had evolved from simple to complex organisms through stages of natural selection. (3)

Declaration on the Rights of Indigenous Peoples adopted by the United Nations in September 2007. This non-binding declaration outlines the individual and collective rights of indigenous peoples, as well as their rights to identity, culture, language, employment, health, education and other issues. (1)

deconstruction an approach (whether in philosophy, literary analysis, or in other fields) which pursues the careful reading of a text. It embraces self-referentiality, which regards the text as a self-enclosed, structural world of knowledge. (3)

Deists believed that religious truth in general could be determined using reason and observation of the natural world alone, without needing faith or organized religion. (4)

economic globalization the increasing expansion of capitalism around the world, integrating non-capitalist economies into a world economic system. Even though countries may have different versions of capitalism, they still participate in the world economy. (5)

economic growth the process by which wealth increases over time as the economy adds new market value to goods and services. It is an essential component of capitalism, which must expand constantly to generate new wealth. (5)

ecopsychology connects psychology with ecology, offers many people a way to spiritually connect with Mother Earth. This emotional connection between individuals and the natural world will help them develop sustainable and simple lifestyles and remedy alienation from nature. (6)

Einstein, Albert (1879-1955) formulated the theory of relativity in 1905, shattering Newtonian certainties and introduced the element of uncertainty: time and space are relative to the viewpoint of the observer and only the speed of light is constant for all frames of reference in the universe. (3)

Evangelicalism the objective was to convert believers to the good news of the Gospel. They wanted a religion of the heart, not the Deist's remote religion of the head. They wanted the faithful to follow biblical authority and to personally commit to Jesus. (4)

fascism a form of authoritarian rule, a radical and authoritarian nationalist political ideology. Germany (Nazis), Italy, and Japan were fascist governments leading up to and during World War II. (3)

financial sector encompasses a broad range of institutions that deal with the management of money. Among these are banks (commercial and investment), credit card companies, insurance companies, consumer finance companies, stock brokerages, investment funds, foreign exchange services, real estate, and others. (5)

fundamentalism a strict belief in a set of principles that are often religious, which is a reaction to perceived compromises with modern social, ideological and political life. (1,4)

Genuine Progress Indicator (GPI) created by the organization Redefining Progress in 1995, measures the general economic and social well-being of all citizens. (6)

global capitalism the dominant economic system in the world, with almost all nations pulled into its economic web. National and local economies, regulated and protected by national and local governments, have been largely folded into one integrated economic system governed by capitalist principles. (5)

Global Wave begins around 2000 and is characterized by rapid technological, intellectual, psychological, spiritual, economic, social, cultural, political, and ecological changes that are profoundly altering familiar patterns of the past. (1)

globalization a complex, multi-dimensional phenomenon that interconnects worldwide economic, political, cultural, social, environmental, and technological forces, transcending national boundaries. It refers to the worldwide compression of space and time and the reduced importance of the nation-state. (5)

globalized worldview has grown out of the modern worldview and has many of its characteristics. In the globalized worldview "time has speeded up" and the pace of growth and development has spread to the farthest reaches of the earth. (1,5)

Hamas a Palestinian political party, faithful to Islam and targets only Israelis who occupy what they and the U.N. claim is Palestinian land. (4)

holistic all the traits of a culture or society—economic, technological, social, political, religious, ideological, and cultural—interact and reinforce each other. (6)

humanism attaches importance to human dignity, concerns, and capabilities, and particularly to reason. (4)

indigenous "from" or "of the original origin." (1,2)

indigenous peoples share a similar ethnic identity and usually inhabit a geographic region with which they have had an early historical connection. (1,2)

indigenous worldview is composed of the outlook and views of indigenous peoples. (1,2)

information specific data or particular services applied to a product, service, or activity that adds monetary value. (5)

laissez-faire **capitalism** or neoliberalism or free market capitalism. In this version of capitalism, government regulations and tariffs were lifted. (3)

LBGT movements have been achieving human rights for lesbian, bisexual, gay, transgender and transsexual people around the world. (6)

liberalism defied the notion of absolute authority by either the church or monarchs. As a result of the political ideas of the Enlightenment, by the 19th century many countries in Western Europe and the United States had adopted some form of representative government guided by a written constitution. (3)

local capitalism reduces dependency on multinational corporations, while creating wealth-accumulating enterprises at the local level. It can produce, market, and process many of its own products for local or regional consumption, reducing transportation and middleman costs and bringing local economies into harmony with the surrounding eco-system, foster cooperation within the community, and substitute more personalized local products for more expensive imported and often sub-standard goods. (6)

Marx, Karl (1818-1882) an early economic theorist, reasoned that human history advanced through stages of development from a feudalistic past, to the middle stage of capitalism, and then finally on to the pinnacle of human achievement: communism. (3)

Menchu, Rigoberta an indigenous person who grew up poor in Guatemala and fought for the rights of indigenous peoples. She won the Nobel Peace Prize in 1992 and was instrumental in the passage of the International Year for Indigenous Populations in 1993. (2)

modern relating to present and recent time and not ancient, remote, or obsolete. (3)

modern worldview traces its history back more than 500 years to the expansion of Western European power and influence around the world. It has been especially powerful over the last two centuries and has today expanded to the farthest reaches of the world. (1,3)

monogamy one spouse, the normative marriage form in the West, expresses democratic, egalitarian ideals in reaction to inequalities and hierarchies often found in polygamous marital societies. (3)

multinational corporations (MNCs) have services in at least two countries, a form of ownership of capital in the global economy. MNCs have maneuvered to gain access and authority over the international rule-making institutions like the World Bank, World Trade Organization (WTO) and International Monetary Fund (IMF). (5)

nation-state the preferred political structure of liberal governments. Great Britain, the United States, and later France pioneered the new political entity, which became the accepted government structure. (3)

neoliberalism or free market capitalism. In this version of capitalism, government regulations and tariffs were lifted. (3,5)

New Age movement emerging out of the West in the 1960s and 1970s, an umbrella term that embraces an eclectic array of spiritual beliefs and practices. It encompasses a wide range of personal development strategies and healing tactics to improve human well-being. (6)

non-governmental organizations (NGOs) privately created organizations with an international scope, unaffiliated with a particular nation. (6)

outsourcing contracting out of a business function to an external provider, usually to a low-wage country. (5)

philosophes during the Enlightenment, they argued for rational, written constitutions to limit the monarch's power and to ensure certain individual rights and equality before the law. They revered, above all else, reason, progress, objective thinking, and the optimistic idea that humans could be perfected through state-sponsored education and a rational society. (3)

post-modern literally means after the modernist movement, but it is generally seen as a point of departure from or a rejection of the modern worldview. (3)

Protestant Reformation starting in 1517, Martin Luther led fervent Protestant religious sects to break away from the all-powerful Catholic Church. (3)

Quth, Sayyid (1906-1966) subjected to physical and mental torture in Egyptian prisons and became radicalized to Muslim fundamentalism. He was appalled with secularism. (4)

Renaissance "rebirth," beginning in Italy, it was a renewal of Greco-Roman civilization and celebrated a new attitude of individualism. (3)

Scientific Revolution around 1500 it challenged the religious thinking of the time and instead celebrated the wonders of the scientific method and reason. (3)

Scopes Trial John Scopes, a young teacher in Dayton, Tennessee, confessed that he had broken the law forbidding the teaching of evolution in the classroom in July 1925. A trial was set. The new American Civil Liberties Union (ACLU) sent a team of lawyers to defend him, headed by the rationalist campaigner Clarence Darrow. When William Jennings Bryan agreed to speak in defense of the anti-evolution law, the trial ceased to be about civil liberties and became a contest between religion and science. (4)

Second Great Awakening (1800-35) a new kind of preacher who stirred up a wave of revivals. The leaders were not educated men, and their rough, populist, democratic Christianity seemed far removed from the Deism of the founding fathers. (4)

secularism the principle of the separation of government institutions and persons mandated to represent the state from religious institutions and religious dignitaries. (3)

shaman is a healer who traditionally performs religious rituals, healing ceremonies, and guides the practice of ancestor worship in traditional societies. (2)

sharing economy takes a variety of forms, often leveraging information technology to enable individuals, corporations, non-profits and government with information to efficiently distribute, share, and reuse the excess capacity in goods and services. (5)

Smith, Adam (1723-1790) the founder of free market economics, in which the "invisible hand" of the open marketplace would set prices according to the principles of supply and demand. This economic thinking emerged out of the liberal political traditions. (3)

social movements steady, incremental progress of the inclusion of legal, political, and other rights of those discriminated against to win greater inclusion into mainstream society. Movements include civil rights, feminism, Native American rights, environmental protection, LGBT rights, people with disabilities, and others. (3)

socialism an economic system in which the government owns and operates large industries such as military, education, transportation, health care, utilities and others, while small businesses are privately owned and operated and citizens can own private property. (3)

state capitalism a system in which the state plays the role of leading economic actor and uses markets primarily for political gain. State capitalist governments believe that public wealth, public investment, and public enterprise offer the surest path toward political stability and economic development. (5)

sustainability is a concept of resource preservation that is more compatible with the indigenous worldview than with the modern. (2)

syncretism occurs where traditional people have blended their indigenous religious/spiritual beliefs with one of the universal religions. (2)

theory of relativity formulated by Albert Einstein (1879-1955) in 1905, shattered Newtonian certainties and introduced the element of uncertainty: time and space are relative to the viewpoint of the observer and only the speed of light is constant for all frames of reference in the universe. (3)

transformative worldview diverse people are actively challenging the negative parts of the four other worldviews. They say a different worldview or a different story is needed to make sure our human species and life as we know it on Earth continue. Leaders from diverse fields – religious leaders, students, entrepreneurs, international political leaders, indigenous farmers, political activists, environmentalists, entertainers, scientists, working people, artists, writers, academics, educators, economists, concerned citizens, and others – are contributing to this worldview. (1,6)

worldview a way of understanding or a lens through which one explains events, phenomena, and actions that happen in our everyday lives. It refers to the framework of ideas and beliefs through which an individual interprets the world and interacts with it. (all chapters)

Zionism a religious form of extreme nationalism or ethnicity, a Jewish movement that arose in the late 19th century in response to growing anti-Semitism in Europe and focused its nationalistic fervor into the founding of a Jewish homeland in Palestine. (4)

Index

sustainability 7, 10, 24-25, 82

T

technology 10, 17, 19, 32, 42, 50, 60, 62, 65-67, 70, 72, 74, 83, 86, 100
theory of relativity 10, 41, 97, 100
Transformative Worldview 9-10, 41, 72-77, 79-81, 83-84, 86-88, 100

V

van Gogh, Vincent 42

Z

Zionism 54, 100

About the Author

Dr. Denise R. Ames is an educator with over 30 years teaching experience at secondary schools, universities, a community college, adult educational programs, and professional development workshops. She took her bachelor's degree in history education from Southern Illinois University, and master's degree and doctorate in history education with a focus in world history from Illinois State University. Her teaching topics range from academic subjects such as world history, global issues, United States history, Western Civilization, world humanities, cultural studies, and global business issues, to secondary social studies classes, pedagogy, and current topics such as global issues, the global economy, global education, and global awareness.

Dr. Ames is currently the founder and President of the Center for Global Awareness, a non-profit organization developing books and educational resources from a holistic approach and global perspective for students and educators in grades 9 through university. Her extensive travels, personal experiences, reflections, and scholarly research have all contributed to her common sense approach to the often overwhelming subjects she teaches and writes about. She is dedicated to working with educators, students, and the general public to foster a better understanding of the myriad of global issues we face, a holistic teaching model for world history, and the effects of the global economy on ourselves, the global community, and the environment.

Dr. Ames is also the founder of the Global Awareness Adult Conversation and Study Program, or Gather. Its mission is to enhance adult learners' global awareness by offering conversation materials that holistically present significant global topics using a unique four dimensional approach called SEEK: see, evolve, engage, and know. By participating in this inspiring conversation program, adult learners will be able to see different perspectives and views, know more about significant global topics, evolve positive attitudes and shift behaviors, and engage more actively in helping to solve pressing global concerns through interacting more deeply with others.

Dr. Ames has presented numerous classes, workshops, and lectures on her holistic world history, the global economy, cross-cultural understanding, and global awareness locally, nationally, and internationally. In addition to her latest book *Five Worldviews: the Way We See World*, she is the author of *Human Rights: Towards a Global Values System*, *Waves of Global Change: A Holistic World History* (2nd edition), *Waves of Global Change: An Educator's Handbook for Teaching a Holistic World History*, *The Global Economy: Connecting the Roots of a Holistic System*, a brief edition of *The Global Economy*, and *Financial Literacy: Wall Street and How it Works*. She has also written numerous blogs, lesson plans, articles, and teaching units for the Center for Global Awareness.

World cultures and history have been Dr. Ames' life-long interest and study. Her extensive travels have taken her throughout the United States and to many international locations. Her destinations include (in order of most recent with year) Croatia (2016), Greece (2016), Slovenia (2016, 1996), Spain (2016, 2006), France (2016, 2006), Italy (2016, 2006), Bahrain, United Arab Emirates, Qatar (2015), South Korea (2014), Germany (2014, 2013), China (2011, 1991), Turkey (2011), Iran (2007), Mexico (2007, 1974, 1967), Singapore (2006), Malaysia (2006), Syria, Lebanon (2005), Costa Rica (2005, 2001), United Kingdom (2000), Israel, Palestine (1999), Galapagos Islands (1999), Ecuador (1999), Russia (1998), Caribbean Islands (2014, 1996), Hong Kong (1991), Austria, Czech Republic, Slovakia, Hungary, former East Germany (1990), Soviet Union (Russia, Ukraine, Moldova, 1989), Brazil, Argentina (1988), Netherlands, Belgium, West Germany (1983), and Canada (many times). Most of her travel experiences focused on historical, economic and cultural developments in the particular country.

Along with her professional interests and work in history, global issues, and education, Dr. Ames has owned her own small retail business for eight years, constructed and remodeled eight houses, and exhibited and trained Arabian horses. She has two adult children, their spouses, and three grandchildren. She particularly enjoys traveling, hiking, yoga, reading, biking, gardening, and visiting with family and friends. She and her husband Jim currently reside in the University of New Mexico north campus area in sunny Albuquerque, New Mexico, USA.

Made in the USA
Lexington, KY
24 August 2019